Your
Child's
Faith

7/98

Building a Foundation for

Your Child's Faith

Dr. Larry D. Stephens

Director of the Minirth Clinic, Richardson, Texas

ZondervanPublishingHouse
Grand Rapids, Michigan

A Division of HarperCollinsPublishers

Your Child's Faith
Copyright © 1996 by Larry Stephens

Requests for information should be addressed to:

📖 ZondervanPublishingHouse
Grand Rapids, Michigan 49530

Library of Congress Cataloging-in-Publication Data

Stephens, Larry, Dr.
      Your Child's Faith / Larry D. Stephens.
         p.   cm.
      Includes bibliographical references (p.   ).
      ISBN: 0-310-20203-5 (pbk.)
        1. Children—Religious life.   2. Parenting—Religious aspects—Christianity.
I. Title.
BV4571.2.S735   1996
248.8'45—dc20   96-24800
                                                          CIP

Printed in the United States of America

---

96 97 98 99 00 01 02 03 /❖ DH/ 10 9 8 7 6 5 4 3 2 1

This book is dedicated to all of the children
who will live in the twenty-first century

Table of Contents

Acknowledgments

First, I would like to acknowledge three of the leading scholars in the field of faith development: Dr. James Fowler, Dr. Juanita Hart, and Dr. Theodore H. Dowell. Without the research and development they conducted years ago, the completion of my contribution would never have materialized.

In addition, I would like to acknowledge my editing staff at Zondervan, particularly Sandra Vander Zicht and Rachel Boers for their work in making such a complicated subject so clear to the parent raising today's child. Thanks, too, to Jim Denney for collaborating with me on the development of the manuscript. His contributions to my work continue to be valuable.

Finally, I would like to acknowledge and thank my wife for sacrificing the love and time she could have received during the thousands of hours spent on this project. It is my prayer that God would bless her one hundredfold for her sacrifice.

ONE

Parenting in an Age of Crisis

IS THERE ANYTHING ELSE I can do to help, Mom?" asked Hanna, bringing the last stack of plates into the kitchen.

"Oh no," said Joanna Brown, taking the plates and setting them in the sink under running water. "You've done far too much already! A young woman in your condition shouldn't be carrying—"

"Mother, please," Hanna interrupted. "I'm pregnant—not an invalid!"

"You're very pregnant, Hanna dear," replied Joanna. "Our first grandchild is due in just a few weeks—and I want to make sure you take good care of him. Or her."

"I am, Mom, I promise. I'm just glad I got to help you with the Thanksgiving dinner this year. Next year it'll be my turn to host the big family gathering, and I want to make sure to remember all the Brown family traditions. The decorations, the place mats, the salad with the marshmallows and fruit cocktail—" Hanna paused, listening.

Out in the living room, voices were being raised. Angry voices.

"That's your father and Michael!" Joanna said in a stricken voice. "What on earth are they arguing about?" She quickly dried her hands on a dish towel, then dashed out of the kitchen, headed in the direction of the voices.

Hanna was in no condition to dash, but she followed as quickly as she could, arriving in time to see her mother step between her father, J. W. Brown, and her nineteen-year-old younger brother, Michael. "What's going on out here?" demanded Joanna.

Moments before, aunts and uncles and cousins had been in various parts of the house—the living room, the dining room, the family room—watching the football game, talking politics, or gossiping, trying to take their minds off how full they felt after a big Brown family Thanksgiving dinner. Suddenly everyone was crowding doorways or looking up from chairs or peering around lamps to find out what the big ruckus was all about.

"Our son," shouted J. W., facing his wife but jabbing one long finger in Michael's direction, "says he's not coming home for Christmas this year!"

"Dad," Michael pleaded, clearly embarrassed, "could we go outside and talk about this?"

"We always have our entire family home for Christmas!" J. W. continued. "But this year our son wants to spend his Christmas away from his family!"

"Dad, please!" Michael groaned. He looked pleadingly over at his sister. Hanna desperately wished she could fix the situation— but once her father lost his temper like this, it was usually best to ride out the storm until his anger was spent.

"Maybe ...," Mrs. Brown said hesitantly, glancing around and noting how uncomfortable her guests were becoming, "maybe it *would* be a good idea for the two of you to talk about this outside."

"I asked him," J. W. continued hotly, seeming not to hear any voice but his own, "why he wouldn't be able to spend Christmas with his family. I thought maybe he had a new job. Or a girlfriend. But no! Do you know why he's not coming home for Christmas this year? Because he wants to spend Christmas alone in his dorm!"

Joanna turned her most wounded look on Michael. "Son," she asked, "is this true?"

"Mom, I—" Michael stopped, looked around at all the staring relatives, then asked again, "Couldn't Dad and I just talk this over outside?"

J. W. rolled his eyes. "Okay," he said gruffly. "Let's go out on the front porch."

As her husband and son left the room, Joanna turned to her guests and said lightly but nervously, "It's okay, everybody. You know how teenagers are. J. W. will straighten everything out."

Hanna felt her husband, Scott, come up behind her and put his arms around her comfortingly. Scott always knew when she was in emotional pain, and he always knew just what to do for her. As she leaned against him, as her mother went back to the kitchen, as all the uncles and aunts and cousins went back to their conversations or their football game, Hanna replayed her mother's words in her mind: *J. W. will straighten everything out.*

Hanna loved her father. She respected the fact that he worked hard at being a good Christian and a pillar of the community. But the fact was, Hanna had rarely ever seen her father "straighten everything out." When it came to emotional issues and relationships, J. W.'s approach tended to tangle things up instead.

Hanna worried about what was being said on the front porch. And she had good reason to worry.

Today's World: A Time of Crisis for Christian Parents

OVER THE YEARS, I'VE counseled many parents like J. W. Brown— devout Christians who truly love their kids and have spent years teaching them about God, doing everything possible to pass on their beliefs. Somewhere along the line, something has gone wrong, and one of their children has veered from the faith. Bewildered, hurt, and feeling guilty, these parents come to me, asking, "What did we do wrong? How could our child have turned away from God like this? How could God have allowed it to happen?"

These are difficult times for Christian parents. Until the past few decades, parents could more or less count on society-at-large supporting, encouraging, and reinforcing the same values taught at home. Today, however, we are forced to parent against the grain of society. Our culture today is engaged in a massive attempt to undermine and undo everything Christian parents try to instill in their children at home. From TV and movies to "values-free" educational programs, our children are drenched with messages that contradict the values and faith we try to pass on to them.

We live in a society that increasingly worships self, sex, sensuality, pleasure, money, materialism, and success at any cost. As Christians, we often insulate ourselves in our cozy Christian communities, failing to realize the degree to which our society is changing and deteriorating. We have lost our ability to be shocked by the growing, casual acceptance of lifestyles and sexual practices that used to be shameful and even unmentionable just a few short years ago. These disturbing social trends are not mere fads or "social crazes," like mood rings or bell-bottom pants. Our culture is undergoing radical, fundamental changes—changes that are pushing our backs to the wall as Christian parents. Here are some of these cultural changes.

The Corrosion of the Image of God

While God's *true* image is incorruptible, the image human beings have of him can be—and is being—marred and corrupted by Satan. My previous book, *Please Let Me Know You, God* (Nashville: Nelson, 1993), explored this issue in depth, so I will only give a few examples here. God has been made to seem irrelevant, by the banning of his name from our public institutions and our classrooms. Because parents have a lot to do with shaping the image of God in their children, the increasing prevalence of abusive or neglectful fathers has distorted the mental-emotional image many people have of their *heavenly Father,* causing them to resent him as either a cosmic abuser or as a kind of absent, remote heavenly deadbeat dad.

God is commonly blamed for all the evil and ills of our society, while the operation of Satan and of human free will are ignored. Because of the rise of the cults and the breakdown of a common belief in objective truth, people today feel free to redefine God in any way they choose, according to their experiences, their feelings, what they hear others say, or their own thinking. We live in an age of manufactured, synthetic gods—and the Bible, once the standard of the truth about God, is now ridiculed as obsolete and even laughable. Those who claim to believe the Bible are sneered at and ridiculed. As a result of these and other trends, the windows of our society have become dirty and fogged, so that people can no longer see the clear, pure, brilliant image of the God of the Bible. At the same time that we, as Christian parents, are struggling to scrub the windows so that our children can see God more clearly, the surrounding society keeps throwing buckets of glop onto those windows, making our job that much harder.

The Breakdown of the Family

Factors in the breakdown of the family include: rising divorce rates (due in large part to crumbling values and a decline in the importance of commitment keeping); the deterioration of the male role model and male leadership in the home (due to such factors as male workaholism, feminism, and the welfare state); rising materialism (abandoning the spiritual for the material); changing economic patterns (high costs of housing, insurance, taxes, and so forth), requiring both parents to work outside the home; attempts by society to redefine the term *family* (for example, calling live-in arrangements and same-sex couples "families"); and so forth. Many young people today grow up surrounded by an unimaginable wealth of material things yet live in abject emotional poverty. Their parents, obsessed with careers, with acquiring, with staying busy, leave their children on their own to fill their unmet emotional and nurturing needs with drugs, alcohol, sex, and immoral music. Christians, unfortunately, are not immune to these antifamily forces, and these pressures magnify the difficulty of the already difficult task of Christian parenting.

The Decline of Values

Over the past few decades, the American value system has steadily been bottoming out. There are many areas in which our values have been turned upside down and inside out: Money—once seen as a blessing from God—is now seen as a god to be possessed. Humility and sound character are now devalued in favor of being self-centered and winning at any cost. Regular church attendance, public prayer, and public reverence for God have fallen into neglect or have been deliberately banned. Taking God's name in vain was once considered shameful and intolerable; now swearing is casually accepted in the workplace and in our entertainment media, and no one is offended—but if you mention God in a respectful way in the workplace, you may be reprimanded for "pushing your religion on others." Children, once considered a blessing from the Lord, are now routinely aborted, abused, or neglected. Binding agreements, once made by the giving of one's word, now require carefully drawn contracts and expensive lawyers and litigation to enforce. Moral absolutes, once commonly accepted, are now rejected in favor of moral relativism: "You have your truth and I have my truth. Don't inflict your morality on me."

These ideas and attitudes, which saturate the media our children are exposed to, are aimed at our children's minds—and their faith.

The Rise of Entitlement

All around us, we see signs of a trend toward excessive preoccupation with the self—the sense that "I am unique, I am entitled to what I want, when I want it, and other people and even God exist to serve me." Another word used to describe preoccupation with the self is *narcissism*. Many narcissistic individuals become self-preoccupied as a result of wounds in childhood, or excessive praise by primary caregivers. These individuals actually think God favors them more than others and that he will treat them in a special manner. While we try to build Christlikeness into our children, the surrounding culture tries to squeeze them into a self-seeking, narcissistic mold.

The Failures of the Church

The church, in many quarters, has become secularized, commercialized, compromised, and rocked by scandals. Like the Pharisees of Jesus' day, many people go to church to impress others with their religiosity, which is one source of the common complaint that "churches are just a bunch of hypocrites." The failure of institutionalized Christianity to meet the needs of its people and to relate to people where they are causes many to view the church as cold, uncaring, joyless, and obsolete. Denominational warfare and church politics turn many away from God, and extreme legalism makes God seem harsh, merciless, and unloving. Many children of Christian homes have been driven away from God by the power struggles and fighting they have seen in their parents' churches.

The Rise of the New Age Movement

The New Age movement poses one of the greatest threats of all to the spiritual well-being of our children. It is a noxious stew of spiritual and social doctrines that is poisoning almost all the institutions of our society—politics, sociology, theology, science, medicine, anthropology, history, sports, entertainment, and literature (particularly fantasy and science fiction). This movement has many facets and beliefs, but in essence it promotes the belief that human beings, individually and collectively, have the spiritual power to be their own god. The bottom-line statement of New Age philosophy is "All is One"—that is, everything is part of a vast, interconnected, interdependent cosmos of pure, undifferentiated energy. You find strong New Age influence in the holistic and homeopathic medicine movements, the one-world government and one-world religion movements, the peace movement ("Visualize world peace"), the human potential-motivational movement, and the environmental movement.

Why is the New Age movement so dangerous to us, as Christian parents, and to our children? Because it offers a seductive, pleasing, sweet-sounding alternative to biblical truth that can subvert or prevent a child's decision to accept Christ as Savior and Lord. New Age goals—peace, love, global unity, the brotherhood of humanity—seem so noble and positive. Instead of salvation, the New Age offers enlightenment. Instead of death, heaven, hell, and judgment, the New Age offers successive reincarnations, leading to godhood—the very same offer made by the Serpent in Eden: "You will not surely die. . . . you will be like God" (Gen. 3:4–5). The New Age does away with "outmoded" and "negative" concepts such as sin, responsibility, atonement, and repentance; instead, you are free to be your own god and make your own moral rules.

"I Just Don't Buy It Anymore"

"WELL, IF YOU WANTED to talk to me alone," J. W. growled, "why did you bring it up in a room full of people?"

"Because I thought you could be reasonable," Michael said tartly. "And besides, Reggie's coming by to pick me up in half an hour, and if I don't talk to you now, I'll have to do it over the phone."

"Do *what* over the phone?" It was dark outside and cold, but J. W. scarcely noticed. He leaned back against the porch rail and crossed his arms, and when he spoke, his words came out in steamlike puffs upon the wintry air. "Now, tell me what this is all about," he said. "Why would you rather spend Christmas alone in a dorm room than home with your family?"

"Because I've had it with all the religious stuff, Dad. I don't believe in God anymore, and I just can't be around when—"

J. W. raised his arms. "I can't believe I'm hearing this! Mike, you were raised in a Christian home! You asked Jesus into your life when you were seven years old! Haven't we taken you to Sunday school every week of your life? Didn't we pray with you every night before bed? Why on earth would you suddenly—"

"Dad," Michael interrupted, "I've just come to the conclusion that all this God stuff you and Mom believe in, all this stuff you taught me all these years about Jesus and heaven and hell and prayer and church—I just don't buy it anymore."

"How can you stand there and tell me you 'just don't buy it anymore'? You were a leader in your youth group. You've given your testimony in front of the whole church. You've been baptized. You've memorized Scripture. How can you just throw all that away?"

"Let me ask you something, Dad. Remember what it says in Proverbs 22:6?"

J. W. was stung by the question. "Yes," he responded bitterly. "'Train a child in the way he should go, and when he is old he will not turn from it.'"

"Well, you trained me," said Michael, "but here I am—an agnostic. I guess that just goes to show that you can't believe everything you read in that book."

"So," said J. W., "this means you don't want to be around your family anymore?"

"That's not it, Dad. I love you and Mom and Hanna. I just don't want to be around this place at Christmastime, that's all. I don't want to sing Christmas carols I don't believe in. I don't want to go with you to Christmas Eve service and have to sit through a lot of meaningless rituals and preaching. Christmas is a religious holiday in our family, and I just don't want to be around religion anymore."

Just then a Jeep Cherokee pulled up at the curb in front of the house. The driver honked twice.

"That's Reggie," said Michael. "Dad, I gotta go."

"Son . . . ," J. W. paused. Anger boiled within him—anger mingled with pain, confusion, and fear. Yet he also felt a protective, hurting, father's love for his son—a love he wished he could put into words. Surely there must be something he could say that would reach his son's heart, that would turn him back to God, back to the faith in which he had been raised.

In a flash, J. W. saw Michael not as the nineteen-year-old agnostic that now stood before him but as little Mikey, the seven-year-old boy whose small hands had nestled inside his own large hands the night they had prayed together at the boy's bedside—the night Mikey had asked Jesus into his heart. He saw the little boy's wide, amazed eyes when, after praying, he had asked, "You mean, Jesus lives inside me now?" What had happened to that little boy? What were the words that could bring that little boy back to the simple faith he once had?

But no words came. The silence hung there between father and son for several awkward, eternal seconds.

"Say good-bye to Mom and Hanna for me," Michael said at last. "I'll call you from school." He ducked inside to grab his suitcase, then dashed off down the sidewalk and jumped into the Cherokee. The driver revved the engine and sped away from the curb as J. W. stood and watched them go.

Tomorrow's World: The Crisis Magnifies

WHY ARE ALL OF these moral, spiritual, and social crises arising at *this* particular point in history? Many Bible teachers agree that we seem to be fast approaching the biblically prophesied "latter days." The world is becoming darker and more dangerous, and as I look at the emerging signs, I have to believe that we are on the doorstep of the end times. In Luke 21:10–12, Jesus predicts, "Nation will rise against nation, and kingdom against kingdom. There will be great earthquakes, famines and pestilences in various places, and fearful events and great signs from heaven. But before all this, they will lay hands on you and persecute you." That phrase *but before all this* is an important clue. Even before the end of the age arises, there will be dangerous events, including persecution and deepening moral darkness.

Jesus also warns in this passage that "many will come in my name, claiming, 'I am he,' and, 'The time is near.' Do not follow them. When you hear of wars and revolutions, do not be frightened. These things must happen first, but the end will not come right away" (Luke 21:8–9). We have certainly heard a great deal in the media lately about those who claim to be Christ, and about wars and revolutions. Jesus assures us that these are the precursors to the end. So I believe we can expect world conditions to worsen as these events approach. Some of the issues, forces, and dangers we can expect to arise over the next five to ten years include

- increasing government control
- increasing trends toward global control
- rising spiritual insecurity
- rising assaults on biblical faith

Parenting in an age of crisis is scary business for Christian moms and dads—but we must not be ruled by fear. We must carefully balance a kind of "realistic pessimism" about the world—a recognition that our society is decaying and declining around us—with a kind of spiritual optimism about God's caring, active role in our families and in our world. God doesn't want us to quake in our boots as we face the future. He wants us to take our children firmly by the hand and to step boldly and courageously into the future as believers who know and trust God and who are unashamed to wear his name.

The question before us is not, "Will there be crises in our society and in our families?" The answer to that question is clear: Crises are unavoidable and inevitable, and these crises do have the power to affect the faith and spiritual stability of our children. As Christian parents, the *real* question we face is, "How can our families be prepared to endure the crises that will surely come our way?" We need to know how to grow spiritually secure children, even in an age of crisis, so that the arrows and stones of this anti-Christian world will bounce harmlessly off them, leaving their faith intact.

In order for our children to have that kind of strong experiential faith, we must begin right now to lay a strong spiritual foundation. Tomorrow will be too late. We have to begin *now* to bulletproof them against the attacks of materialism, New Age religion, humanistic government, and anti-Christian social institutions. The human soul cannot stand a vacuum, so we must make sure that there is no spiritual void within our children—or something terrible and deadly will rush in to fill that void. When we instill in our children not only traditions and religious information but a *living, dynamic, experiential relationship* with Jesus Christ, then they will be able to navigate the murky, treacherous waters of the New Age and the new world order that is rushing upon us all.

How do we encourage that kind of experiential trust relationship with God into our children? That is what this book is about.

"I Think I'm Beginning to Understand . . ."

MR. BROWN PICKED UP the phone, punched a few buttons, paused . . . then set the receiver back in its cradle. He cleared his throat, breathed a silent prayer—a hurting father's prayer—then lifted the phone once again. What would he say? What would his son say? He entered the number and waited through the first ring, the second—

"Hello?"

"Mike? Michael, this is your father."

"Oh? Oh, hi, Dad."

"Are you ... Is this ... Did I catch you at a bad time, Son? Do you have a few minutes to talk?"

"Sure, Dad."

"You said you'd call. I waited a few days, then ... well, you know how it is. We parents worry too much, I suppose. Umm ... How's school?"

"Dad, you didn't call to ask me about school."

"No, Michael, I didn't. I guess I don't know where to begin. I just ... I just don't understand what's going on inside you, Son. But I want to understand. I really do."

"There's nothing to understand, Dad. You raised me the best you could. Now I've grown up. You and I just look at life differently now. Why don't we just leave it at that. I don't want you trying to preach to me or convert me. I don't want you laying your Evangelism Explosion training on me or giving me the Four Spiritual Laws. I just want to have my own beliefs, my own way of looking at things—and I want you to accept that."

"How can I accept that?" J. W. felt his voice beginning to quaver, and he fought to control his emotions. "All your mother and I have ever wanted was for you and your sister to grow up knowing Jesus, living in God's will. When you told me you had rejected the faith you were raised in, it was my worst nightmare come true! How can I accept that?"

Anger and defensiveness crept into Michael's voice. "Look, Dad, don't come unglued—and don't try to control my life!" J. W. had never heard that tone in Michael's voice before. It scared him.

"I ... I don't want to control you, Son," J. W. said, lowering his tone. "I really just want to understand."

"You really want to hear it? You may not like it."

"I want to know the truth. You're my son and I love you. But suddenly I feel I don't really know you. I don't want my own son to be a stranger to me. If there is something going on inside you—if there's something I've done to hurt you or to damage your faith in God—I want to know."

"Okay, Dad," Michael sighed. "Here goes.... Do you remember that time—I must have been in junior high, but I remember like it was yesterday—when I asked you how Jesus could actually turn water into wine? I'd just finished my chemistry homework, and I was trying to understand how molecules of plain water could instantly be turned into molecules of sugar, alcohol, and the other stuff in wine. Remember what you said when I asked you about it?"

"It's so long ago. I don't remember the ... What did I say?"

"You said, 'Oh no! You're not going to be like Peter, are you? He doubted the miracles of the Lord, and he sank in the lake and the Lord had to pull him out! And he was so thick-brained that he denied Christ three times! Mike, you're not going to be like that, are you?' And then you walked away. Right then, Dad, I felt so bad, I didn't feel like Peter, I felt like Judas! For a long time I hated myself for asking a stupid, doubting question—but you know what, Dad? I realize now that it was a *good* question, a *normal* question for a teenager to ask—and instead of giving me an honest answer, you made me feel stupid and sinful just for asking. Whoever said 'It never hurts to ask' never met you."

"Now, that's unfair, Mike. How could I give you an honest answer to that question? Am I supposed to know the chemical processes of a miracle?"

"An honest answer, Dad, would be, 'I don't know.' In all the years I lived in your house, I never once heard you simply admit, 'I don't know.' If anyone asked you a question you couldn't answer, you had to make the other person feel bad for asking such a stupid question."

"That's not true!"

"Fine. You said you wanted to understand what's going on inside me, but if you don't want to hear what I have to say, then—"

"No, wait, Son. It's just that ... well, how can this one incident cause you to lose your faith?"

"Come on, Dad, that's just one example! Shall we go through the list? How long have you got? I mean, the whole time I was growing up, you sent me to the church academy. I hated all the rules and restrictions, I hated that stupid uniform I had to wear, and I hated being one of only two junior high kids in the whole academy. I could never go out for sports, because the academy didn't have sports. Do you know what the kids in the neighborhood used to call me? 'The Jesus Geek'!"

"Son, I—"

"And all those rules you made Hanna and me live by, Dad! I mean, you and Mom wouldn't let us listen to the kind of music we like, because Pastor Knight once said, 'The rock beat is the heartbeat of the devil.' There was nothing wrong with my music. I wasn't into anything satanic, none of that heavy metal stuff or even grunge rock. I just wanted to listen to Amy Grant and Mariah Carey, but even that was outlawed in our house. I mean, no wonder all my friends thought I was weird!"

"We just wanted to protect you from the world."

"You smothered me, Dad. You wouldn't let me breathe. You kept me shut up in that church my whole life. We were always the first to arrive and the last to leave—Sunday mornings, Sunday evenings, *plus* Wednesday night prayer meetings and Monday night Bible studies, *plus* youth group, *plus* you even made us go to school at church! My whole life was church, church, church, church, *church!* And you know what, Dad? I *hate* church!"

"I can't believe I'm hearing this. I can't understand what could have happened to your thinking."

"Dad, I've just started thinking. After all those years of sheltered childhood, I've come to this university and I've been exposed to ideas I've never heard of before. I've been reading Camus and L. Ron Hubbard and the Urantia book and *The Way of Zen* and all kinds of stuff. I can't believe how little I knew about the outside world before I came to school here."

"Oh! Now I see! I should have known! It's that university you're going to! I knew we should have insisted you go to a Christian college. Now some godless, atheistic professor has gotten ahold of your mind and turned you—"

"No one got hold of my mind but me, Dad," Michael grated angrily. "I'm figuring out a lot of things for myself. Like the whole thing in Genesis, with six days of creation and Adam and Eve and the Serpent—man, it's all a big crock. And Jonah in the belly of the big fish? I can't believe I fell for that whopper all these years. And the Resurrection? No way, Dad. I'm sorry, but I'm just not buying all that mythology anymore."

"Now, you listen to me, Son—"

"Dad, I spent ninety-nine percent of my life listening to you. I think it's time for you to listen to me for a change. Isn't that what you said you were going to do? Listen and learn? Well, Dad, listen to this: Every person reaches a point where he has to decide if he still believes the things he was taught as a child, if those things still make sense or not. I've thought about these things for a long time—about God, about the way the world is, about the way people are, about what life is all about. I think back on all the miserable, uncaring people I've known at church, on all the conflicts and political bickering that went on at the congregational meetings. Then I look at all my friends, and some are involved in the New Age or scientology, and others are just atheists and agnostics—and they seem really together, compared with that bunch of Holy Rollers you hang out with on Sunday mornings. You and Mom used to warn me about New Agers and cultists, yet I've found out that they're nice people—nicer than a lot of Christians I know."

"Mike, if you could only see what a terrible mistake you're making. Doesn't it worry you to think you might be throwing away your entire eternity with God?"

"You mean hell? I don't believe in hell anymore. I don't see how any rational person could believe that a God of love would ever send people to hell. Maybe there is a God of some sort—I'm not saying there is or there isn't. But I'd rather think of God not as a person but as a power or a force that we can plug into whether we understand it or not. I think the world would be a better place if we could do away with concepts like hell and guilt and sin and morality and a personal God who looks down on us in judgment. It's my business what I want to think, what music I listen to, what movies I watch, and even who I sleep with. It's not your business or God's business. It's my business, do you understand?"

J. W. was silent for several seconds. Then he said slowly, "I think I'm beginning to understand . . . a lot of things. I know you're angry with your mother and me for the way we raised you. I know you feel we've hurt you and deprived you, but I don't know what else we could have done. I think I need to think about what you've told me. I don't know how your thinking has become so distorted—"

"It's not distorted, Dad. I'm thinking clearly for the first time in my life."

"I know you believe what you say. But permit me to have my own opinion in the matter, Michael."

"That's fair."

"Before I go, I just want to say . . . your mother and I both love you. That will never change—no matter what. And we're praying for you, Son."

There was silence on the line.

"Did you hear me, Mike?"

The voice that replied seemed very far away. "Yes, Dad. I heard."

"Good-bye, Son."

"Good-bye, Dad."

The Road Ahead

THERE IS A LOT of pain ahead for J. W., Joanna, Michael, and Hanna. Emotional pain. Relational pain. Spiritual pain.

In the coming pages, we will unpack their pain and examine their stories and the stories of other people. Some of the people we will meet are parents who want the best for their children but don't know how to give it. Others are children who have been raised in Christian homes yet who have grown up with a damaged faith. We will look at some of the mistakes and failures Christians experience as they attempt to raise their children for God. And we will see some of their successes, including their recovery from the sins, mistakes, and regrets of the past. My prayer is that you will learn from their mistakes so that you can avoid those same mistakes in your own life—or if need be, recover from them.

In this book, I will draw from my years of experience as a Christian counselor and share with you what I have learned about spiritual and emotional development and about how you can

- give your children strong, firm spiritual roots
- understand your child's specific needs and the developmental tasks he must complete at each stage of his life
- assess the spiritual growth and development of your child

- repair spiritual damage done to your child earlier in life
- build bridges of trust between your child and God
- choose a healthy church environment for your child's early religious training
- set your child on the pathway to spiritual maturity and security

This book is a book not just to read but to live in and to wrestle with. At the end of the book, in chapter 10, we will take the principles we explore in these pages and apply them to the nuts-and-bolts realities of our lives and our children's lives.

The world of the twenty-first century is a scary place, filled with pitfalls just waiting for our children to tumble into and lose themselves. As Christian parents, we worry about the road ahead and about where our children's steps will take them in the world of the future. Will they remain secure, holding fast to their faith in God? Or will they fold under the pressure? The answers to those questions depend to a large degree on the choices we make today.

My prayer for you as you walk through these biblically based principles with me is that at the end of this book, you will emerge equipped to make the choices that point your children toward a strong, trusting, lifelong, joy-filled adventure with our loving heavenly Father.

TWO

Spiritual Seedlings

Hanna wanted to bear down, to push her little baby out of her body and into the world. But the doctor had told her to wait, to breathe, to resist the almost irresistible urge to push. With her husband holding her shoulders, coaching her exactly as their Lamaze teacher had trained him to, she panted, trying to suppress the pain and her overwhelming urges with every shallow breath.

"All right, Hanna," said the doctor, with the characteristic calm of his profession. "Give me a big push now."

Oh yes! Finally! Grimacing, she put everything she had into a mighty push—and she could feel the pain. But she could also feel her baby moving.

"That's it! That's it!" shouted her husband, who was looking up at the mirror behind the obstetrician's head. "I see him! There's his head! And his shoulders! Oh, he's beautiful, Hanna! He's so beautiful!"

Hanna only had strength to cry out one word: "She!"

Scott understood. "Okay, Hanna. *She's* beautiful."

"Hanna's right, you know," said the doctor, holding up a shiny, pink baby, still trailing a purple umbilical cord. "She's a perfect little girl." As he held the baby, the OB nurse aspirated the baby's mouth and nose with a bulb syringe. The child began to cry.

And so did Hanna. "Oh! She's so pretty! Can I hold her?"

"Of course you can," said the doctor, his eyes smiling above his surgical mask. "She's all yours, after all. Just wait till we get this cord off her and get the placenta delivered. Then we'll clean her up a bit and she's all yours."

"All mine," Hanna said dreamily.

"What's her name?" asked the nurse. "Do you have one picked out?"

"Jenea," said Hanna. "Her name's Jenea."

"Pretty name," said the nurse.

Scott leaned close to Hanna, put his hands around hers, and whispered so that she alone could hear, "Thank you, Jesus. Thank you for this gift of life."

Hanna nodded, eyes glistening, smiling sweetly, listening to the music of her baby's first cry.

A baby is a gift of life, a gift of love. This is true of a little girl named Jenea, born in an American city in the 1990s. And it is even more true of a little boy named Jesus, born in a Jewish village two thousand years ago. Scott and Hanna, loving Christian parents that they are, intend to introduce their little newborn girl to that Jewish baby, the Gift of the first Christmas. They have dreams for their little girl—dreams of an eternity secured by faith in Jesus Christ and by trust in the love of a gracious heavenly Father. But how will those dreams be realized? How can Scott and Hanna make sure that Jenea has every possible spiritual advantage, every possible opportunity to build a strong, durable friendship-and-trust relationship with Jesus Christ?

It all begins—believe it or not—at conception!

Spiritual Growth in the Womb

I AM CONVINCED THAT from the moment of conception, a child has the capacity for spiritual growth. From the earliest stage of life, God knows your child and is already involved in the ordering of his life. The Old Testament talks about God's close involvement in the creation of new life.

> The word of the LORD came to me, saying,
> "Before I formed you in the womb I knew you,
>   before you were born I set you apart."
>
> Jeremiah 1:4–5

And the psalmist writes,

> For you created my inmost being;
>   you knit me together in my mother's womb.

I praise you because I am fearfully and wonderfully made;
    your works are wonderful,
    I know that full well.
My frame was not hidden from you
    when I was made in the secret place.
When I was woven together in the depths of the earth,
    your eyes saw my unformed body.
All the days ordained for me
    were written in your book
    before one of them came to be.

Psalm 139:13–16

Of course, the spiritual reality of an embryo is not something you and I can relate to, but this we can say with assurance: God knows every child from the moment of conception. In accordance with the divine laws of creation, he provides every life with a body, soul, and spirit, with full potential for growth in each domain. All three of these dimensions of a child's life will in time become increasingly important to the child's total spiritual growth. They work together in a beautiful way in the life of a child.

- The *body* that is being formed and developed throughout the nine months of pregnancy is a temple, a dwelling place, for the Holy Spirit.
- The *soul*—which itself consists of three dimensions: will, mind, and emotions—plays a prominent role in a child's spiritual growth. Through the will, the child can one day make a choice for God—or against God. Through the mind, the child can know, learn, and contemplate God and the purpose of his own life. Through the emotions, a child can eventually meet and experience God—not just as an idea but as a personal friend.
- The *spirit* is the part of the child that reaches out to know God. At the point of salvation, the human spirit becomes the medium through which the child can possess the Holy Spirit. This establishes a bond that transcends both life and death.

God has created every child with the potential for total spiritual growth, for a full and satisfying relationship with him. But how could a child's spiritual growth actually occur in the womb? After all, the child does not understand language and cannot directly communicate with his parents. Yet there are fascinating indications that faith development begins even before birth. Harvard-trained theologian and developmental psychologist James Fowler conducted ten years of research on faith development and coined the term *primal faith*. In 1980, when asked in an interview for an article about the stages of faith that children go through, he said, "Let me first mention primal faith, not a stage per se, but very important. It is rooted in prenatal time and infancy. The mother's frame of mind during pregnancy and those who are closest to her have an impact on the formation of the child."[1]

Though skepticism is understandable, the suggestion that different levels of prenatal communication can occur between an unborn child and both parents has been well documented in scientific and medical journals for years. In one study on prenatal attitudes of parents toward their children, the experimenter evaluated two different groups. One group was made up of well-adjusted, happy children; the other group was made up of troubled children. The results: those children who grew up well-adjusted and happy had parents who maintained a healthy, positive attitude during pregnancy.

Can children who are still in the womb actually sense whether or not they are loved? According to nationally recognized behavioral pediatrician Paul Warren, "studies and experiments indicate that they do indeed. Your child knows before birth how you feel about him. From conception your attitude counts."[2]

One way of understanding the relationship between an unborn child and his parents is from the perspective of systems theory. This is the theory that teaches that every living organism is part of a bigger whole that exists around it. To fully understand how the organism behaves, we must understand the system of which it is a part. In a system, every part of the overall system is affected by every other part, either directly or indirectly.

Putting this in human terms, each individual person is a member of a system called a family. When your child is conceived, he is instantly a living being, a part of your family system, possessing the ability to interact with every other part of that system. The baby, even while in the mother's womb, has an effect on the total system.

Here are some examples of the dynamics that operate when an unborn baby enters the family system: The unborn child changes the mother's body chemistry. The beat of the child's healthy heart has a calming effect on the mom who listens intently for it. When the baby stirs or kicks, mother and father become moved and excited. Any motion or interaction from the unborn child brings a swell of joyful emotion to the parents. The child also receives stimulation from the parents. When they place their hands on the mom's abdomen, the child senses the presence of someone outside his cozy world. The child can hear and respond to the gentle voice of the mother's prayers and singing—or the harsh sounds of an argument. In the womb, the child receives first impressions of the environment he is soon to enter.

What is taking place here is the beginning of a real relationship between a tiny, unseen life and the two adult lives who sustain and care for it. Here we have the first stirrings of what James Fowler calls "primal faith." In the womb, the child forms a deep sense of trust and security, and learns a rudimentary form of relatedness to his primary caregivers. In a healthy child raised in a healthy family system, these are the same bonded feelings that, according to God's plan, are later transferred to the relationship between an individual and his heavenly Father. Even though the relationship between child and parents is extremely primitive and immature at this stage, the relationship is real. Impairment of this relationship (due, for example, to extreme conflict, dysfunction, substance abuse, or other emotional problems in the family system) can lead to impairment of the child's later ability to experience a rich and satisfying relationship with God.

It may be, however, that you were not a Christian when your child was in the womb, or you were extremely dysfunctional at that time. Maybe you went through bouts of depression or experienced a lot of conflict during your pregnancy. This doesn't mean your child's spirituality is impaired for life. The prenatal stage is just one of many stages that affect your child's spiritual health.

The point is that this relationship between you and your child begins not at birth but nine months before. You can have a powerful effect on the course of your child's life, starting as soon as the pregnancy begins. You can enhance your child's ability to experience a healthy faith relationship with God, by building a strong, secure trust relationship with your child right now—even if that child has not yet been born. The effects you produce in the experiences and sensations of your unborn child are small—but they accumulate. Added to all the other positive ways you can influence your child, from birth to young adulthood, these small effects can add up to a major influence on your child's future, including his *eternal* future.

A Page from Hanna's Diary

HANNA SWITCHED ON THE light by her hospital bed. In the soft glow, she could see Scott sprawled in a chair at the foot of the bed, snoring softly, his head lolled back. He stirred slightly when the light clicked on, but did not awaken. Quietly Hanna reached for the little leather-bound book on the nightstand, opened the metal clasp, and took the pen from the pocket inside the cover. Flipping to the middle of the book, she found a blank page and began to write.

> December 5, just before midnight
>
> Praise God, our little Jenea was born at 8:17 this morning! She's so precious and beautiful—a little angel with invisible wings. She has little wisps of brown hair and dark brown eyes. At least, I think her eyes are brown—she hardly opens them long enough for me to see. She's so tiny—only 6 lbs. 5 oz.—yet she is a special, complete individual, the object of God's love.
>
> Twelve hours of labor—I was so exhausted! I slept most of the day, except when they brought Jenea to me for feedings. My milk's not in yet, so Jenea's not getting anything— but I do love holding her close and talking to her. She's in the nursery now, and Scott's asleep in a chair nearby. I guess I

spent too much of the day asleep, because now it's almost midnight and I'm wide awake! But at least I have a chance to write down a few thoughts in this diary.

I remember going to visit my cousin Kathy a year ago when she was eight months pregnant. She used to sing and pray out loud and talk to the baby inside her. At first I thought it was kind of strange—but soon I realized what a wonderful, bonded relationship Kathy was building with her baby, long before the baby was out of the womb. I'm so glad I had Kathy's example to learn from, because I've been able to experience that same kind of relationship with Jenea these past few months as she's been growing inside me.

Jenea seems to know my voice—as if she knows that this person who holds her and hovers over her is the same one whose voice she has listened to through the walls of her world for the past nine months. What does Jenea think and feel when she's close to me? How aware is she of her mommy, her daddy, her surroundings? I wish I knew—but I'm sure she's more aware, more in touch with her world, than anyone realizes.

Scott and I put our hands on Jenea and prayed over her today. We want nothing more than for her to grow up knowing Jesus as her Lord and Savior and Friend. I want to do everything right for her. I think of what's happened to the faith of my brother, Mike, and I think of some of the mistakes Mom and Dad made with us when we were growing up. They meant well, they tried to raise us in the faith—but some of their good intentions went awry, especially in Mike's life. I just hope and pray that we will do the right things in Jenea's life!

Oh, Lord, please give us wisdom as parents. Please help us to clearly portray your loving character to Jenea as she grows up. Hold her tightly in your hand and never let her go. We dedicate our little girl to you, Lord, and trust you to mold her life and shape her spirit—in the name of your Son, Jesus.

P.S. And Lord—please heal the hurt and restore the faith of my brother, Mike.

Ministering to an Unborn Child

No ONE CAN SAY with scientific certainty how much spiritual and emotional input a child is able to receive as a toddler, a newborn, or an unborn child. But as Christian parents, we should want to do everything possible to spiritually nourish our children and to prepare ourselves spiritually for the task of guiding and raising our children to know and love God. I don't believe that any ministry we do for our children is ever wasted—even ministry we do for them before they are born. Here are some suggestions for acts of ministry you can do for your child, both before and soon after your child is born.

Pray. Pray audibly for your baby. Ask God to nurture your baby's body, soul, and spirit as he grows in the womb. As we have seen in the Psalms, God is involved and active in your child's prenatal life, from the moment of conception.

Maintain a positive mental attitude. Meditate on God's goodness and his love for your child. As much as possible, try to eliminate stressful conditions from your life. Some stressful situations are unavoidable, of course, so seek God's perspective on those situations and ask God to help you not to worry or feel anxious. He is in control, and he will bring you through whatever you are facing. By keeping your mind and emotions focused in a positive direction, you avoid stirring up the physical responses (such as changes in hormone levels, heart rate, and blood pressure) that are not helpful for either you or the baby.

Listen to good music. Christian music awakens the spirit within us, which is why God tells us in Ephesians 5:19, "Speak to one another with psalms, hymns and spiritual songs. Sing and make music in your heart to the Lord." You cannot see or touch an unborn child, but your child can hear your voice and sense the peace and serenity that music brings to your own soul. Your unborn child is a living spiritual being, and living spiritual beings respond to music.

Read the Bible. Read God's Word and meditate on his comforting truth for your own life and the life of your child. Read aloud so that your child can share the rhythms and cadences of

God's Word, even though he cannot grasp the words. As God ministers to your spirit through his Word, the trust and serenity you feel will minister to the spirit of your child.

Walk in the Spirit. In other words, live daily in a trusting, faith-filled, obedient relationship with Jesus Christ. Allow your mind and emotions to be controlled by God's Spirit rather than by circumstances or moods. Most pregnant mothers are careful not to take anything into their bodies that would contaminate or harm their child; it is just as important not to take any contaminating agent into our mind and spirit during that time. As the Lord tells us in 2 Corinthians 7:1, "Let us purify ourselves from everything that contaminates body and spirit, perfecting holiness out of reverence for God."

Truth Paves the Way for Healing

HANNA SAT UP IN bed, cradling Jenea in her lap. Mother and daughter had only been home from the hospital a few hours when their first visitors arrived: Hanna's parents—Jenea's grandparents. At this moment, Scott was out in the kitchen, helping Hanna's mother prepare lunch, leaving Hanna and her father alone to visit together.

"Would you like to hold her, Dad?" asked Hanna, lifting the little pink bundle from her lap.

"Me?" exclaimed J. W. "Oh, these big, clumsy hands are likely to break a fragile little thing like her."

"You won't break her, Daddy," laughed Hanna. "You held me plenty of times when I was a baby, and you didn't break me!"

Suddenly a cloud seemed to pass over J. W.'s face. Hanna eyed him closely. Were those *tears* she saw in her father's eyes? They were! In all the years she had lived under her father's roof, she had *never* seen him cry before. "Dad," she said worriedly, "what is it?"

"You said I didn't break you, Hanna," said J. W., his voice choking with emotion. "I wonder. I think I broke your brother, Michael—broke his faith, that is. Maybe I broke yours too."

Hanna lifted Jenea close to her face, rocking her gently. "Oh, Dad, don't say that."

"It's true," said J. W., sitting down heavily in a chair near the bed. "I've done a lot of thinking since your brother told me he wanted nothing more to do with Christianity. Hard thinking. Soul-searching. Remembering. This whole thing with Michael has shaken me to the core of my being. I realize now that the only person to blame for your brother's broken faith is me."

"Oh, Daddy . . ."

"And I realize I hurt you too."

"What are you talking about?"

"It's all been coming back to me. All those times you doubted your salvation. All those nightmares you had when you were a child. Hanna, how many times did you raise your hand or go down the aisle to be saved and re-saved and re-re-saved?"

"Oh yes, I remember," said Hanna, nodding. "I must have been 'saved' a hundred times or more. I was always afraid I didn't ask Jesus into my heart the right way. What if I didn't say the right words? What if part of me didn't really mean it? I kept needing reassurance that God would accept me. I used to worry a lot about going to hell. But I don't blame *you* for that." Hanna bit her lip, knowing that the last statement had been a lie, and knowing that the lie had been perfectly transparent to her father. Of course she had blamed her father for the problems in her faith—but she had long ago forgiven him, and she had never wanted to talk about it, for fear of hurting him.

"Don't you blame me, Hanna?" said J. W. "Who's to blame for the problems in your faith and Michael's faith if not me? Why do you suppose you felt so insecure all those years? Why did you worry that God would not accept you? Why were you so scared that you might not have said just the right words to please God? Didn't I make you feel insecure? Could it be that you felt I didn't accept you? Did you feel you had to be careful around me, that if you didn't do and say everything just a certain way, I might jump on you, get mad at you? Didn't I drill the fear of God into you much more than the love of God?"

"Daddy, I . . . I don't know what to say."

"Because it's all true, isn't it?"

Hanna was silent for several moments. "Suppose it is true. Suppose you were too harsh, too legalistic, with Mike and me. Maybe that explains my doubts. Maybe that explains what Mike is going through right now. But whatever happened, whatever your imperfections as a parent, you loved the Lord and you loved your children. You wanted what was best for us, and you did the best you could."

"Good intentions are not enough," J. W. groaned, two glistening tear-tracks running slowly down his craggy features. "If I lose my own son, Hanna—if Mike never returns to the faith—then what?"

"I don't believe God is going to let go of Mike."

J. W. shook his head slowly. "I don't know, Hanna. I just don't know." He sighed deeply, then looked up at his daughter—and his new granddaughter. "But I do know this: little Jenea is going to be all right. I've watched you these past nine months, Hanna. I've seen the way you have loved and cared for that child even before she was born. It's a beautiful thing, Hanna, and you've taught me something about how to love a child, how to teach a child about God's love. I was never very good at showing God's love to you and Mike when you were children. Maybe it's not too late to change that. Maybe if I can just love Michael the way God loves him—who knows? Maybe I can reach him."

An Awesome Challenge

HOW DOES GOD PROVIDE for the spiritual growth of a child? Through the child's parents. Our task, as Christian parents, is to provide the nurturing a child needs to grow strong in a trust relationship with God. When we demonstrate love, grace, affirmation, and forgiveness to our children, we demonstrate the character of God to them. When we build a strong sense of security into our children, they grow up feeling secure in their family, in their lives, and in their relationship with God.

You are God's representative, divinely ordained by him to portray and exemplify his life and character to your child, from the moment that life is planted, like a spiritual seedling, in your family.

Even before conception, God knows your child, and from the moment of conception forward, your child depends on you and relates to you. Christian parenting is an awesome challenge—the most overwhelming yet rewarding challenge you will ever confront.

Something eternal comes into existence at the moment of conception: an individual soul, a human spirit. And from that moment on, this spirit never ceases to search for God and his love. Your task, long before this child is born, is to point this tender little spirit toward the light of God.

THREE

The Power of a Parent's Spiritual Character

MㅤICHAEL SMILED BROADLY—A LITTLE too broadly, thought Hanna—as he slid into the booth at Laredo's. He seemed ... well, perhaps he seemed nervous and apprehensive. Usually Hanna could read her younger brother like a book. Today it was hard to know what was going on behind his smiling-yet-troubled eyes.

"You look great, Hanna!" said Michael. "Already got your figure back and everything!"

"Liar!" laughed Hanna. "But thanks for saying so, anyway. I'm still twelve pounds heavier than I was before this one came along." She patted little Jenea, who sat perched on the restaurant table, strapped into an infant seat.

"She's grown since I saw her last," said Michael. "She looks like you, Sis. Very pretty. How old is she now?"

"Four weeks. And she still hasn't figured out yet that the nighttime is for sleeping."

Just then the waiter arrived with menus, plus a server bearing a large basket of tortilla chips and a bowl of salsa. "I've never eaten at Laredo's before," said Michael. "What do you recommend?"

"Well, my favorite is the seafood enchiladas in heavy cream sauce."

"Sounds rich!" said Michael. "What about your girlish figure?"

"You just never mind about my girlish figure, Brother dear," Hanna retorted with mock annoyance. "Scott's going to be so jealous when he finds out I had lunch here without him. His favorite is the steak with roasted garlic and hot peppers. It's so hot and spicy, he's sick all the next day—but he can never resist it!"

"I think I can resist it. I'll take the seafood enchiladas."

Hanna eyed him closely. Behind all the small talk and bantering, Michael was edgy about something. She was sure of it. "Mike," she said, her forehead lined with concern, "is something bothering you?"

"Bothering me?" Michael's eyebrows raised. "No, nothing's bothering me! . . . Well, maybe, in a way . . . I mean, it's just that . . ." His hesitation grew into an awkward pause.

"What is it?" Hanna prompted.

"I guess I'm just wondering why you invited me out to lunch. You've never done that before. I guess I'm a little afraid you're going to . . . well, you know . . . preach to me. Try to convert me."

"No," said Hanna. "I just wanted to have lunch with you. I wanted to check in with you and see how you're doing. If you want to talk, I'm willing to listen, and if you don't want to talk, that's OK, too."

Michael looked back at his sister through dark, troubled eyes. He was silent for a long time. Then he said, "Yeah, I think it might help to talk."

"Good," said Hanna. "What do you want to talk about?"

"Mom," said Michael. "I want to talk about Mom."

The Spiritual Character of Mothers

AS A CHRISTIAN COUNSELOR, one of the most common questions I hear from mothers is, "How much influence do I really have on my child's spiritual growth?" The answer: More than you'll ever know. And the influence you have on your child takes place not only through what you do but, even more importantly, through *who you are*. Simple Christian character is a much more critical factor than all of the parenting techniques and methods contained in a thousand books on parenting.

Spiritually committed Christian mothers have helped to lay the early foundations for many of the world's great leaders. Through the children they have raised, these Christian mothers have influenced millions of people and changed the course of history. One such mother was Morrow Graham, mother of evangelist Billy Graham. In his biography of Billy Graham, William Martin writes,

> When Billy Graham's parents married, they dedicated their union to God, reading the Bible and praying together on their wedding night, and keeping the "family altar" each night in their home. The primary impetus for that practice seems to have come from Billy's mother, Morrow Graham. Morrow drummed Bible verses into Billy's head as she scrubbed his back in the washtub; fittingly, the first one she taught him was that great golden test of evangelism, John 3:16. She also kept a Scripture calendar on the breakfast room wall, and each morning she tore off a verse the children were expected to memorize.[1]

Where would Billy Graham be today if not for the early spiritual influence from his godly mother?

No greater example of godly womanhood and motherhood can be found than that of Mary, the mother of Jesus. At first glance, you might think that the differences between you and Mary, and between your child and her child, are so vast that you simply can't relate to her as an example. In fact, however, there is much we can glean from Mary's life that will serve as an excellent, inspiring, practical example to Christian mothers today. I am convinced, from my study of Scripture, that Mary had a profound influence on the spiritual development of her son Jesus. God could have chosen any woman in the world to bear his Son—a world-famous queen or a harlot in the street. I believe God chose Mary, a quiet, simple country girl with strong, obedient faith, because God wanted his Son to grow and develop under the nurturing influence of a humble, faithful, devout mother.

Jesus did not suddenly appear on the scene at Bethlehem, preaching to crowds and performing miracles. He came as a baby, helpless and dependent, and grew as a boy, moving through the developmental stages that are common to all boys—stages of physical, mental, emotional, and spiritual growth. As Luke 2:52 tells us, "Jesus grew in wisdom and stature, and in favor with God and men." The early life of Jesus was characterized by growth and development under the godly nurturing of his mother, Mary.

As a baby, Jesus was circumcised and presented to the Lord on the eighth day, just like any other Hebrew boy. Throughout his boyhood, Jesus was subject to the authority of both Mary and Joseph. Though he displayed an astonishing level of understanding as a twelve-year-old (he amazed the teachers at the temple in Jerusalem with the depth of his questions), he remained humble and submissive to his parents. After amazing the scholars, Luke 2:51 tells us, Jesus returned to Nazareth with his parents "and was obedient to them." Though the deity of Christ is absolutely real, this passage from the early life of Jesus shows that his humanity is equally real. The parents of Jesus played an influential role in his life, and that gives us a powerful reason for examining the parental model and spiritual character of Mary.

What kind of mother was Mary? She came from a family line with a strong spiritual heritage. According to the royal genealogy found in Matthew, and the human genealogy of Luke, Mary was of the tribe of Judah and the line of David. Her own godliness and obedience, demonstrated in Mary's song to God (Luke 1:46–55), are indications that she was brought up in a knowledge of the Scriptures and in a spiritual atmosphere of great faith and continual prayer. When she was visited by an angel announcing that she had been chosen among all women to bear the Savior, the angel said to her, "Greetings, you who are highly favored! The Lord is with you" (Luke 1:28). Since God is clearly pleased with Mary and since it is impossible to please God without faith, we can assume that Mary was a godly woman of faith who came from a family with a very strong faith.

Was Mary a perfect parent? I would doubt it. I'm sure she made her share of mistakes. But on the whole, it seems that her first concern was always to be available and obedient to God. As Dr. Herbert Lockyer writes in *All the Women of the Bible*,

> The woman who was to give him birth, whose breast
> would be his pillow and who would nurse and care for him
> in infancy, who would guide his steps through boyhood

years, and surround him with true motherly attention until his manhood, had to be a sanctified vessel for the Master's use.[2]

The home of Mary and Joseph was not a dysfunctional home, as so many American homes are today. Reading between the lines of Mary's story—her love and obedience to the Lord, her caring and concern for Jesus, the obvious kindness and gentleness of her husband, Joseph—suggest that this was a family in which there was continual affirmation, unconditional love, discipline without shaming, and spiritual instruction by example. It is easy to suppose, given what we know of Mary's mothering style, that she believed in spending time with her child, sharing fun while teaching wisdom; that she enthusiastically answered the child's curious questions about life and read stories to him out of the Scriptures; that she affirmed him, cherished him, prayed for him, comforted and consoled him. This is the kind of family heritage in which God wanted Jesus to be raised.

Humility, faith, godliness, obedience, and a courageous commitment to undergo hardship in order to carry out the will of God and to raise her son for the Lord: these are the qualities that characterized Mary, the mother of Jesus. Two thousand years later these are still the qualities necessary to meet the most basic spiritual needs of a child. The same qualities that enabled a boy named Jesus to grow up spiritually secure in his world are no less needed by children of our own world today and of the world tomorrow.

Unfortunately, while the spiritual needs of children have not changed in all these centuries, the values and attitudes of our world have changed dramatically. All too many Christian women have bought into the false "You've come a long way, baby" attitudes of the late-twentieth-century culture. Many mothers today are more concerned with boosting the family finances or boosting their own self-esteem than with securing the faith and spirituality of their children. Here are some of the contrasts between the attitudes of Mary and the attitudes that pervade the world of today's woman.

Mary's Attitudes	Today's Attitudes
1. Right and wrong are clear	1. There are no absolutes
2. Faith in God	2. Faith in self
3. Beauty is based on character	3. Beauty is based on appearance
4. Humble and submissive	4. Proud and autonomous
5. Pursue eternal wisdom	5. Pursue the latest fad
6. Value righteousness	6. Value political correctness
7. Wife-mother role comes first	7. Self-fulfillment comes first
8. Respect parents	8. Disregard or dishonor parents
9. Seek obedience	9. Seek "my rights"
10. Trust God completely	10. "God makes mistakes"
11. Suffering and sacrifice produce growth	11. Seek pleasure and material gain
12. Patience is a virtue	12. "I want it all and I want it *now*"

I am not saying that a wife must be only a wife and homemaker, that no mother should ever work outside the home, that no mother should have outside interests or a career. The most powerful and detailed description of godly womanhood is found in Proverbs 31, and there you find the positive qualities listed above—and more! It is important to note, by the way, that the description of a godly woman found in this passage was written not by a man but by a *woman:* the mother of King Lemuel. While the godly woman described in Proverbs 31 places her role of wife and mother first, she is also involved in the real estate business, plus she is engaged in gardening (v.16).

> She considers a field and buys it;
>> out of her earnings she plants a vineyard.

She operates a small business and works long hours to make it a success. She has a strong Protestant work ethic (vv. 17–19).

> She sets about her work vigorously;
>> her arms are strong for her tasks.
> She sees that her trading is profitable,
>> and her lamp does not go out at night.

In her hand she holds the distaff
    and grasps the spindle with her fingers.

She is generous in giving time and substance to those who are in need (v. 20).

She opens her arms to the poor
    and extends her hands to the needy.

But amid all these activities, her first and foremost concern is always for her family (vv. 27–29).

She watches over the affairs of her household
    and does not eat the bread of idleness.
Her children arise and call her blessed;
    her husband also, and he praises her:
"Many women do noble things,
    but you surpass them all."

Obviously, there are variations from woman to woman, family to family, situation to situation. Not all women have the time or the strength to handle a family plus a side business or separate career. For such women, the godly decision is clear: put family first. If you have no time for other things after meeting the needs of your family, then you should not be dabbling in real estate or working in an office.

Some women—forced by circumstances they did not create—must take on the role of family provider and be away from their children for large parts of the day. Single mothers should not feel guilty for doing what they have to in order to provide for their children. In such cases, a career outside the home is clearly not just a matter of self-fulfillment; it is putting your children's needs first.

"Mom and Dad Were Not Perfect Models"

"WHAT ABOUT MOM?" ASKED Hanna.

Michael sighed. "I know this whole thing with me has been hard on Mom. How's she doing?"

"Well, you know Mom. She has her ups and downs."

"Yeah. That's what I was afraid of."

"She's real happy to be a grandma. That takes her mind off . . . other things."

"Does she ever get like she used to?"

"You mean, all those bouts of depression she used to go through?"

Michael nodded. "I remember one time, coming home from school and finding the house completely dark, all the shades drawn, and Mom sitting in a chair, just staring. I tried to talk to her, but she wouldn't answer. It was as if I didn't exist. Hanna, I got so scared."

"I know. I remember trying to convince Dad that he needed to get some help for Mom—professional help. But he kept saying, 'What would people think? What would that do to our family's Christian testimony?' So we put on our Sunday smiles and pretended to be the perfect Christian family. And when Mom was too depressed to go out of the house on Sunday mornings, we'd just tell people she was sick."

"She was sick," said Michael bitterly. "She needed a doctor. But Dad was too proud to get her the help she needed, so he just let her suffer. He let us all suffer. I remember going to Sunday school and singing songs about the joy of being a Christian, then coming home with those songs still echoing in my ears, and seeing my mother sitting in a gloomy, dark house, a cloud of suicidal depression hanging over everything. That's when I started to see that the Christian faith just doesn't square with real life."

"Oh, Michael, that's just not true," said Hanna. But seeing Michael stiffen in his chair as she said that, she quickly said, "But I'm not here to argue with you. I understand how you feel. The fact is, Mom and Dad were not perfect models of what the Christian life was meant to be, and you were hurt by that."

"Not perfect? They were miserable models! I mean, Mom was always emotionally out of the picture, and Dad was physically gone all the time. He was so busy with church—serving on every committee, teaching a Sunday school class, acting as a deacon or elder—yet he seldom came to one of my Little League games, never took me camping. I only remember one real family vacation we ever took, and it was obvious Dad couldn't wait to get back home and get back to his church meetings. Did you know that he never sat me down and had that talk with me that dads are supposed to have with their sons? About the facts of life and what it means to be a man and all that?"

"Every boy needs attention and affirmation from his father," said Hanna. "I'm sorry you never got that. You must have felt so alone."

"I felt abandoned—as if he didn't care about me. As if there were something wrong with me."

"Maybe," Hanna said tentatively, breathing a silent prayer that Michael would take her next words to heart, "your feelings of being abandoned and rejected by Dad have something to do with your feeling that God is remote and impersonal. You grew up in a household where what you saw and what you were told about God didn't make sense—so maybe right now you're trying to make your own god—a god that will make sense to you."

The waiter picked that moment to arrive with their order. Michael seemed lost in thought, hardly noticing or acknowledging as the food was set before them. Finally, after the waiter left, he looked Hanna in the eye and said, "Maybe you're right. Maybe I am looking for a God who makes sense. But what's wrong with that? What's wrong with wanting to believe in something that makes sense? It doesn't make sense to me that a loving God would send people to hell just for not having the right set of beliefs. It doesn't make sense to me that a good God would create a perfect world and then allow sin to come into it and fill it with misery and hate. I'd much rather believe in a God who is imperfect, or a God who has gone away, or a God who is impersonal and is just the sum total of all the laws of the universe, than believe in a God like Mom and Dad believe in."

"Do you hear what you're saying, Mike?"

"What's that?"

"You said, 'I'd much rather believe in' this or that kind of God. Unfortunately, what we'd rather believe in isn't always what is. Sometimes you have to accept reality, whether you'd rather believe in it or not."

"So who says the God of the Bible is reality?"

"That's something you have to sort out for yourself. But I want you to sort it out *honestly*. What I see going on inside you is a rebellion."

Michael bristled. "That's a lot of—"

"Just let me finish," Hanna continued. "I see you rebelling against an image of a demanding and controlling God because you were raised by a demanding, controlling father. You look at the gods of the New Age movement and you see a very lenient, flexible image of God—a God who makes no demands on you, a God you can control instead of a God who controls you, a God you would rather believe in. What is it they say in *Star Wars*? 'Trust your feelings.' Well, your feelings can betray you, Mike. Trusting your feelings is not a good way to choose your eternal destiny."

There was defensiveness in Michael's eyes. "I thought you said you weren't going to preach to me."

"I'm not preaching, Mike," said Hanna. "I haven't quoted Scripture or tried to convince you that Jesus is the way or that you're going to hell if you don't repent. Not once have I told you what you should believe. I just want you to be intellectually honest about what you believe. Don't choose your religious faith on the basis of what you'd rather believe in. Don't make a decision based on rebelling against the way you were brought up. The fact that Mom and Dad were imperfect doesn't automatically mean God is imperfect. If I were you, I wouldn't simply reject Christianity out of hand just because that's the faith you were raised in. I'd lay it out alongside all the other competing faiths and give it a fair shot."

"I was raised in a Christian home," Michael responded with a dismissive gesture. "I think I've given Christianity a fair shot for all these nineteen years."

"No, you haven't," Hanna said flatly. "Most of that time, you superficially accepted what you were taught by Mom and Dad. Then, at a certain point, you turned around and rejected it just as superficially. I think you owe it to yourself to take a hard look at the faith you were raised in. Read some C. S. Lewis and Josh McDowell and others who can explain the rational underpinnings of Christianity. Most important of all, just take a year to read the Bible from cover to cover. See for yourself if it makes sense or not."

"And if it doesn't?"

Hanna took a deep breath. "Then at least you'll know what you're rejecting."

The Spiritual Character of Fathers

GOD HAS PLACED THE primary leadership responsibility for the family on the shoulders of the father. But even more than that, God has placed on fathers the responsibility to *model godly character* to their children and to raise their children to be emotionally healthy rather than filled with anger and bitterness. In *What My Parents Did Right*, Gloria Gaither gathers memories of several well-known Christians as each reminisces about what his or her parents did right.

James Dobson recalls,

> The very happiest days of my growing up years occurred when I was between ten and thirteen years of age. My dad and I would rise very early before the sun came up on a wintry morning. We'd put on our hunting clothes and heavy boots and drive twenty miles. After parking the car and climbing over a fence, we entered a wooded area where we would slip down to the creek bed and follow the winding stream several miles back into the forest.
>
> ... The intense love and affection generated on those mornings set the tone for a lifetime of friendship. There was a closeness and a oneness that made me want to be like that man ... that made me choose his values as my values, his dreams as my dreams, his God as my God.
>
> James C. Dobson, Sr. was a man of many intense loves. His greatest passion was his love for Jesus Christ. His every thought and deed were influenced by his desire to serve his Lord. And I can truthfully say that we were never together without my being drawn closer to God by simply being in my dad's presence.[3]

My research shows that one of the most crucial factors in a healthy image of God is the consistent childhood experience of unconditional love and nurturing from parents or other primary caregivers. In other words, if we, like James Dobson, had fathers who were positive, affirming, and nurturing—fathers who built our sense of self-worth and made us feel confident and loved— our image of God would tend to be accurate and consistent with who God really is. However, those of us whose fathers *failed* to model God's loving and accepting nature are much more likely to suffer a distorted image of God.

I remember a counseling session I once had with a young man named Tom. At our previous session, I suggested to him that he come prepared to talk about his spiritual life. Now he seemed nervous and fidgety. I asked my first question: "Tom, are you a Christian?"

He responded with intense, edgy defensiveness. "Yeah," he said, "I guess you could say I'm a Christian—depending on what you mean by the term."

"Okay," I said, "tell me about your spiritual walk."

"You mean, do I go to church?" I could practically reach out and grab the invisible chip on his shoulder. "No," he stated defiantly. "You don't have to go to church to be a Christian."

"If you mean that going to church doesn't make you a Christian," I said, "then I agree with you. Living in a garage doesn't make you a car, and sitting in a church doesn't make you a Christian. Church, by itself, can't save anyone."

Tom relaxed a bit when he heard that.

"However, there is a passage in Scripture," I continued, "Hebrews 10:25, I believe it is, that says, 'Let us not give up meeting together, as some are in the habit of doing, but let us encourage one another.' Church doesn't save us, but it does encourage us in the things that produce salvation and a more satisfying life."

Tom frowned. "I know about that verse, but I've learned you can't take everything in the Bible literally. I don't get any encouragement out of church. Churches are just full of hypocrites, anyway."

"So you don't have much use for churches," I said. "Knowing the bickering and power politics that take place in some churches, I can't say that I blame you for feeling that way. But the fact is, we're not free to pick and choose what parts of the Bible we would like to obey and what we would like to discard. We pretty much have to take the whole enchilada. Maybe with a little investigation, even with a little help from me, you could find a church that isn't full of hypocrites. You might even find a church with the kind of music you like to listen to and a pastor who can really relate to the kinds of issues you go through every day."

"Well, I've tried churches before."

"How many?"

"A lot."

"What's a lot? Thirty or forty?"

He shrugged.

"A dozen?"

He looked away.

"Two or three?"

"Something like that."

"Fact is, Tom, there are a lot of churches out there, and you haven't tried them all. All this talk about hypocrites in the church is just a worn-out excuse for sleeping in on Sunday mornings. That dog don't hunt, Tom. It's time to be honest with God and with yourself."

Tom's head lowered and his face darkened. For a moment, I thought he was getting ready to fly into a rage. Then came the real shocker: Tom *agreed* with me! "Dr. Stephens," he said, "you haven't told me anything I didn't already know. I just needed to face it." Then he began to pour out his story. "The real reason I hardly go to church or read my Bible or pray since I left home," he explained, "is my dad. He never beat me or anything terrible like that, if that's what you're thinking. But in almost every aspect of his life, he was two-sided. His public image and the real guy were two different things. In church he portrayed himself as this big Righteous Joe, and everybody looked up to him, even kow-towed to him. Behind the closed doors of our house, my mom, my brothers, and I knew what he was really like. He liked to control things. He controlled all of us in his family. He was sort of the unofficial boss in that church, so he controlled the pastor and all the programs of the church."

"What was your dad's personality like?" I asked.

"To me, he was cold and distant—though he could also fly into a rage when you weren't expecting it. He never had much to say to me unless he really got mad. Nothing I did was ever good enough to please him. I always wondered why he was so warm and charming and smiling to strangers, yet so bitter and nasty to his own family. He was very hard on my mom—always criticizing her appearance and everything she did."

"It must have been hard," I said, "seeing your father get away with his pious act every Sunday, when you knew all the time that it wasn't real."

"There were times I sat in church and fantasized about going up to the front, grabbing the microphone off the pulpit, and telling everyone in church what a phony my dad was. I often wish I'd had the guts to do it. I guess I kind of consoled myself with the idea that my dad wasn't unusual, that all Christians are phonies. Deep down I knew it wasn't true, but it made me feel better if I could just write the whole church off." He paused, as if he had more to say but wasn't sure if he should say it.

"What else, Tom?" I prompted.

"Well, there was another deep disappointment in my life when I was around sixteen. Our pastor was a really nice guy—at least he seemed to be. He was always real kind to me—affirming, an encourager. He really reached out to me when I was going through some tough times at home and at school. Then, all of a sudden, it came out that he was having an affair with a woman in the church. He resigned from the pulpit, and there was a story about it in the newspaper and everything. It was horrible. I didn't even get to say good-bye or talk to him or anything. He was just ... gone. He had been kind of a substitute father to me, since I couldn't talk to my own father—and then he let me down like that."

"That must have been really painful, Tom," I said.

"Yeah," he said glumly, his eyes seeming to stare far away. Then he looked at me. "Dr. Stephens," he asked, "are there any truly godly men in the world anymore? Is there anyone you can really count on?"

"There's no one who's perfect," I said. "Any human being can make a mistake or commit a sin and let you down. But there are Christian men who really do set a goal of being true spiritual leaders in their homes. There are a lot of men in churches who are sincere in their faith and who really want to be the same in private as in public."

"I want to be like that," said Tom. "I want to be a good Christian, through and through, and I want to be a good father to my own kids."

———

LIKE SO MANY PEOPLE I have counseled, Tom had come into my office with a broken image of God—an image of God and an attitude toward God's church that were largely shaped by his father. All of us, to some degree, gain part of our image of God from our fathers. In other words, we project our mental image of our father onto God. If you had a warm, secure, nurturing relationship with your father, you are more likely to have a warm, secure, nurturing relationship with God. If your relationship with your father was bitter, painful, and stormy, your relationship with God will likely reflect that. The father's role in shaping his children's spiritual development is boldly underscored by both clinical experience and Scripture. As Ephesians 6:4 tells us, "Fathers, do not exasperate your children; instead, bring them up in the training and instruction of the Lord."

Our image of God may also be a projection of our mother image or the image of another significant caregiver in our lives—or some combination of these various images. But having counseled hundreds of people who struggle with distortions in their image of God, I am convinced that the most significant parental projection in most people's lives is that of their *father*. Other adult figures certainly have an influence on a person's image of God in positive and negative ways, but the father seems to hold the key to the developing mind of a child when it comes to shaping that child's image of God.

Once Tom was ready to recognize and admit the truth about how his father had helped to distort his perception of God and relationship with God, he was ready to break the cycle and begin the healing process. Many fathers like Tom go through their entire lives in denial, never experiencing a close, meaningful relationship with God and never allowing themselves to be the spiritual leaders in their homes. Their children are the true victims. Tom's own children will now have the chance to experience a stable spiritual foundation.

The Spiritual Character of Joseph

THE FATHER OF JESUS was God the Father, and we see that clearly in the way Jesus prays and continually addresses God as "Father." But Jesus had an earthly guardian, or stepfather. His name was Joseph. We know little about Joseph, because he fades out of the gospel accounts after Jesus turns twelve. Perhaps he passed away during Jesus' teen years; had he been alive, he almost certainly would have been mentioned more often, as Mary was (significantly, she is present in the gospel accounts from before the birth of Jesus until the scene of his death upon the cross).

Though we know little about Joseph, the few things we do know are important and revealing. He was a carpenter, the son of Heli, from the line of David—certainly not a wealthy or distinguished man. How did the Lord come to choose Joseph as the earthly guardian for his Son, Jesus? We find one clue in Matthew 1:19, which tells us that "Joseph . . . was a righteous man." When Mary was pregnant with Jesus, it appeared that she had committed sexual sin and had been unfaithful to her husband-to-be, Joseph. He would have been within his rights to have her publicly shamed, yet the Scriptures tell us he was a righteous man and did not want to expose her to public disgrace. In the context of the culture, to be righteous meant to be known as a person of high integrity. He took his faith seriously and he lived it. No one would find him living a double life.

Joseph obviously knew the true meaning of authentic unconditional love, and he demonstrated it toward Mary. When he learned she was pregnant, Joseph did not do what one would have expected in that culture. Instead, he handled the situation by thinking of Mary's needs, not his own wounded pride or the pain of (as he must have thought) having been betrayed by his bride-to-be. It is important to note that he demonstrated this loving attitude even before the angel came to him, announcing the miracle of the Virgin Birth.

The most distinguishing aspect of Joseph's spiritual character was his profound obedience to God, exemplified in Matthew 1:24: "When Joseph woke up, he did what the angel of the Lord had commanded him and took Mary home as his wife." There was no hesitation or questioning in Joseph—just simple, faithful obedience.

As a father, you may not be another Joseph—and your kids are certainly not Jesus! But we can keep the model of Joseph before us. As fathers, we can set before ourselves the goal of being men of righteousness, integrity, authentic love, and obedience. We can seek to be men of Christian character—not men who are two-sided and double-minded but men whose outer reputation is seamlessly joined to a sterling inner reality. We can seek to be men who will project all the character qualities of God to our children through our own godly lives.

The Fruit of the Spirit

AS PARENTS IN TODAY'S society, facing a new world, a new age, a new century, we need to do a bigger and better job of being spiritual leaders—better than we are currently doing, better than our parents did, better than our parents' parents did. Why? Because as we saw in chapter 1, our children will grow up in a different, more dangerous, more pressure-filled world than we did. Our children will face tougher obstacles to their faith development than you or I have had to face in our lifetime.

God has created the potential for total physical, emotional, and spiritual growth within each child. For each child, he has provided parents to direct this growth, and he expects us, as parents, to fulfill our roles and to be positive forces in their development. But we can't be powerful spiritual forces in the lives of our children unless God is a powerful spiritual force in our own lives. Our own spiritual condition—individually, as parents, and as marriage partners—is absolutely vital to the planting of our children's earliest spiritual roots.

God's provision for the spiritual growth of a child is completely mediated through his parents. Nowhere in the Bible does God ordain anyone else but mom and dad to carry out that awesome responsibility. Your child, being physically immature and helpless, depends on you for the provision of food, clothing, and shelter—the things that are necessary for physical life. In the same way, your child, being spiritually immature and helpless, depends on you to provide for his spiritual needs, to model the character qualities of Christ, to build a trusting and secure faith in that child—in short, to provide all the things that are necessary for spiritual life.

Your child systematically and unknowingly adopts your character qualities and coping style. When you are faced with dilemmas and challenges, your children observe both your good, healthy choices and your sinful, unhealthy choices. With their own little eyes and through their own real-life encounters, your children watch to see whether you actually live out your faith, whether you abide by your own teachings, whether you truly seek God first.

Wearing the title *Christian* does not automatically qualify you to be a good parent, nor does it guarantee that you will raise a spiritually secure child. Many of the worst parental horror stories I've seen have come from "Christian" homes. It takes more than good doctrine to be a good Christian; it takes character and consistency. It takes the fruit of the Spirit, which are listed in Galatians 5:22–23: love, joy, peace, patience, kindness, goodness, faithfulness, gentleness, and self-control. These are called "fruit of the Spirit" because they are the sweet, nourishing outgrowth of a life that is controlled by the Spirit. They are the outward evidence of the inward change and growth that Jesus Christ is gradually producing in our lives—if we are completely surrendered to him. And they are the fruit we can expect to see in our own children as they model themselves after the life of God that they glimpse in us, from infancy to adolescence and beyond.

What's Real and What Isn't

"YOU'RE RIGHT, SIS," SAID Michael, holding the door for Hanna as she stepped out of the restaurant, carrying Jenea in the infant seat.

"Oh?" she said. "About what?"

"About giving Christianity a fair shake," said Michael. "I have to be honest with you. I don't think my mind is going to change. But I intend to take one last, hard look at the Bible before I completely turn my back on it."

"That's fair."

Michael stopped walking and looked Hanna squarely in the eye. "I just don't want to be forced into some religious mold anymore, you know?"

"I know, Mike."

"Now that I'm on my own, going to college, encountering new ideas, I just want to be myself, an individual with my own thoughts, my own questions, my own opinions, my own impulses. I don't want to suffocate inside the religious comfort zone of my mother and father."

"Fine. Make your own decision, Mike. A well-thought-out, honest decision. That's all I ask."

"I will," said Michael. "Look, Hanna, I don't really believe in it anymore, but ... well, would you pray for me? Pray that I'll know the truth when I see it? I really do want to know what's real and what isn't."

"Sure, I'll pray for you, Mike. You can count on it."

———

THERE IS MORE TO the story of Michael and Hanna, of little Jenea, and of Mr. and Mrs. J. W. Brown. Much more. In the next chapter, we will look at the role that family traditions and spiritual heritage play in the formation of a child's faith.

FOUR

Defective Traditions

J. W. WAS *HOVERING*. THAT'S the only word Scott could think of to describe it. While Scott basted the Thanksgiving turkey in the big gas-fired barbecue on the back patio, J. W. stood around, watching worriedly, offering "suggestions" (which sounded more like criticisms), and muttering under his breath.

"That's an interesting way to cook a turkey," Mr. Brown observed. Scott smiled to himself. He knew that *interesting* was the word J. W. used when he wanted to show disapproval without being too obvious about it. Of course, J. W. was about as subtle as a Mack truck. Though Scott had only been married to Hanna for about three years, he had learned how to deal with his father-in-law's intrusiveness: smile, thank him for his interest—and don't let him get to you.

"I think you'll really enjoy this bird," Scott replied genially. "My dad taught me how to smoke a turkey. He was a master at it."

"It's always been kind of a Brown family tradition to roast a stuffed turkey in the oven," J. W. observed.

"Know what you mean," said Scott. "Tradition's a wonderful thing. 'Course, there's a lot to be said for trying new experiences."

"I suppose," said J. W., without conviction. There was a long silence, and then he added, "Maybe we shouldn't have put such a burden on you and Hanna—hosting the Brown family Thanksgiving. After all, it's a big responsibility, and you two being so newly married, with a baby not even a year old yet—"

"Oh, I think we can handle it all right. Hanna's got the rest of the meal under control. Joanna has the table all set and decorated. Everything's going to be just fine."

Mr. Brown muttered something.

"Pardon me?" asked Scott.

"Hm? Oh, nothing. Nothing."

Your Spiritual Heritage

ONE QUESTION I HEAR over and over from concerned, conscientious parents is, "When is a child ready to start learning about God?" My answer: The task of teaching a child about God begins a generation or two before the child is born. And I'm absolutely serious about that. Traditions are important in any family—especially spiritual traditions. Customs, attitudes, and habits passed down from generation to generation can have a profound effect on the spiritual welfare of our children—for good or for ill.

Sometimes parents and grandparents pass down healthy and positive models of God—they are an accurate, biblical reflection of who God is and what it means to know him. All too often, however, a family's spiritual heritage is transmitted with misconceptions and distortions that hinder the youngest generation's ability to fully know and experience a satisfying relationship with God. Frequently parents and grandparents pass down not the *reality of a relationship* with God but the *form of religion*: a set of rules, rituals, and legalistic formulas without personal, meaningful, useful spirituality. The spiritual heritage that is handed down to our children is like the soil in which they put down roots. If it is good, fertile soil, their roots will grow deep and strong. If not, their roots are much more likely to dry up and wither away.

I once counseled a woman we'll call Sheila, who told me about the spiritual heritage she had received. "My mom and dad were separated a lot, so I spent much of my childhood at my grandfather's house," she recalled. "He was a very religious man, and he tried to make up for the lack of positive spiritual influence in my home. He used to teach me about the Ten Commandments, and by the time I was six, I could recite them from memory—even though I didn't have a clue what 'Thou shalt not commit adultery' meant. Grandpa would say, 'Sheila, you remember those commandments, and don't you ever break them, if you don't want the Lord to get mad at you.' I sure was scared of the thought of God being mad at me. After all, Grandpa told me that God is everywhere, he sees everything, and he won't let any sins go unpunished."

The constant battles Sheila witnessed between her mother and father while she was growing up made the little smattering of religion she got from her grandfather seem unreal and shallow. "I saw the commandments my grandfather talked about so much being broken every day," she explained. "By the time I left home, got married at age nineteen, and had my first child at twenty, God didn't mean anything to me. Go to church? Completely point-less. Pray? Who would I pray to?"

But then, after her marriage failed, something happened that changed Sheila's perspective on God. "I met this guy, a really ter-rific guy," she said. "We dated, and he did the strangest thing on our dates: he witnessed to me! Instead of trying to compromise my virtue, like all the other men I dated, he was actually inter-ested in me, in my eternal future, in my happiness. He told me one thing that really startled me. 'Sheila,' he said, 'I like you, and I think I may even love you—but I could never marry you if your heart didn't belong to Jesus.' I said, 'What does religion have to do with being in love with someone?' And he quoted me this verse in the Bible about being 'unequally yoked' with someone. I didn't understand it at all, but I did know one thing: this guy was very serious about his Christian faith. And that made me begin to think seriously about what I believed and what I was living for."

Soon Sheila gave her heart to Jesus—and about a year later she and this young Christian man were married. "My husband, Carl, is the most wonderful man in the world," she says, "and the reason for that is, he came from a spiritually healthy home. He was raised in a family in which he learned what it really means to have not a religion but a *living relationship* with Jesus Christ."

Carl's rich spiritual heritage has been grafted into the life of Sheila, a woman with a distorted and feeble spiritual heritage. She has learned much from Carl, and she is continuing to learn and grow in her relationship with Jesus Christ. But equally (if not more) importantly, Carl's spiritual heritage is having a profound effect on the growing faith of Sheila's daughter by her previous marriage, Mandy. "My daughter is just starting junior high,"

Sheila explained, "and she's going into that war zone—with all the drugs and fast boys and pressures and all—with a good foundation, thanks to Carl. I shudder to think where Mandy and I might be heading right now if not for the firm foundation of Carl's strong faith and spiritual heritage."

What about the teaching she received as a child from her grandfather? Didn't it help her to learn the Ten Commandments at such an early age? "If anything, the weak injection of religion I received from my grandfather probably inoculated me against ever catching real faith in Christ," Sheila says today. "Hearing about God from Grandpa, then seeing the way my parents used to claw at each other, probably did more to undermine my faith than anything else ever could have. It was only the overruling grace of God that brought Carl into my life so that Mandy and I could have a personal relationship with Christ and experience God's love."

Sheila is living proof of the devastating intergenerational effects of an extremely flawed spiritual heritage on one's spiritual growth. But Sheila's story also shows that intergenerational distortions about God do not have to continue generation after generation. We can break the cycle. We can find healing in our spiritual heritage, and we can pass on a truer, more realistic faith experience to our children.

No Marshmallows in Cool Whip This Year

"BUT WE ALWAYS HAVE oyster bread dressing with Thanksgiving turkey!" Joanna Brown exclaimed.

"I know, Mom," sighed Hanna, "and we always have tons of oyster bread dressing left over because most people in our family hate oysters. I hate oysters. Scott hates oysters. I called all my cousins and polled them, and they all hate oysters."

"I don't like oysters myself," said Joanna, "but I serve them and I eat them. It's a Brown family tradition."

"Not this year, Mom." Hanna lifted the lid from the big Corningware baking dish and revealed the contents. "See? Apple and onion dressing. You'll love it."

Joanna gasped. "Apple and onion dressing! What is your Aunt Elma going to say? You know how she hates onions!"

"So she can have an extra helping of mashed potatoes."

"Oh, dear. Well, at least let me help you make the salads."

"The salads are all made, Mom."

"Where's the ambrosia salad?"

"The what?"

"Ambrosia. You know, the salad we have every Thanksgiving, with the marshmallows, the fruit cocktail, and the Cool Whip in it? It's a Brown family tradition. I gave you the recipe."

"Oh yeah. I decided not to have that this year. Or any of the other traditional salads."

Joanna gasped.

"I'm trying some new salads this year—kiwis and cranberries in orange Jell-O, a jalapeño coleslaw, and a green salad with pine nuts and radicchio. Who knows? Maybe we can start some *new* Brown family traditions."

Joanna sat down. She looked pale.

"Mother, are you all right?"

"Oh, Hanna, Hanna . . ."

A Tradition of Internalized Faith

I'LL NEVER FORGET BROTHER Bob, my youth pastor when I was eleven or twelve years old. I can see him in my mind's eye as clearly today as if he were standing in front of me. What was so memorable about Brother Bob? He had a powerful impact on my faith and my spirituality, even though I don't recall us ever having a Bible study together or memorizing Scripture together or doing many other things one usually associates with "spiritual" or "religious" pursuits. Brother Bob was not just my pastor; he was my friend. And it was his friendship—not his teaching or preaching ministry—that made the most powerful impact on my life.

At age eleven, I hardly knew what the words in the Bible meant. But I did understand what it meant to have a friend and to be affirmed. Whenever Brother Bob saw me, he seemed genuinely happy to see me. We played tennis and he took me out to breakfast.

He must have given me a thousand "atta-boy's." If he had to be tough on me, he surrounded his toughness with a sense that he believed in me and wanted me to live up to my potential—and he always forgave instantly. He was not afraid to be physical with me, giving me a firm handshake, a pat on the back, a bear hug, or a man-to-man punch on the arm. A touch tells a person, "I want to be close to you. You're okay."

Now that I am an adult and have studied human nature and psychology for a number of years, I realize what Brother Bob was doing. Either intentionally or instinctively, he was filling a deep void within me I didn't even realize I had at the time. Though my own father was a good Christian, a good provider, and a kind father, I did not really feel close to him when I was growing up. I needed a father figure to feel close to, and Brother Bob filled that role for me. As a fatherly friend, Brother Bob had a greater influence on my spiritual growth than he probably realized.

Did my parents provide spiritual instruction and a nurturing environment for my faith? Absolutely. Our family practically lived at church when I was growing up. My mother was a Sunday school teacher, plus she was in the choir and directed all of the church social banquets and events. My dad was even more involved. He often wore the "hats" of various church roles at the same time: choir member, substitute song leader, church treasurer, deacon, Sunday school teacher, bus driver—he even went to church on Saturdays and cut the grass! My parents were extremely dedicated to their church and to serving the Lord. The faith environment they created for me had a profound impact on my early spiritual growth.

Yet despite all those years of church activity and church involvement, my encounter with Brother Bob for the few short preadolescent years of my life continues to pervade and illuminate my memories of the church I grew up in. He influenced me in ways I continue to experience to this day. He shaped my early impressions of God, spirituality, and Christian lifestyle—and he did so without teaching or preaching. He did so by simply being a good friend.

Brother Bob taught me a lot about the crucial—and frequently overlooked—role of the personal, relational element in developing and deepening a child's faith. He helped me, perhaps more than any other adult influence in my early faith development, to *internalize* my faith. It is crucial that we understand the role of internalizing faith in our children.

Most of what we do as parents, pastors, and Sunday school teachers is to impart the externals of the Christian faith to the children in our care. We give information. We tell Bible stories. We preach doctrines. We have kids memorize Scripture verses. All of that is good—but these are all external experiences of Christianity. It is data, not experience. In order for faith to be truly internalized and made an integral part of a child's life, that child must experience faith in a personal, emotional, meaningful, experiential way.

Although we can experience and internalize God on an ongoing basis throughout our lives, the most basic and formative foundations of trust are laid down in the first two years of life. During those first two years, we learn to count on our primary relationships—first with our parents and later with God—to meet our needs. People who may not have experienced a sufficient degree of internalized parental nurturing and love may have difficulties feeling secure and trusting toward God. In extreme cases, in which there has been neglect, abuse, abandonment, or loss of parents, the ability to internalize God may be severely impaired. Lacking the emotional security and trust that God intended us all to have, these individuals often encounter problems in their faith development: distorted images of God, an inability to trust God, an inability to commit to God and obey him, a wariness or resentment or unnatural fear toward God, a sense that God is remote or absent, a sense that God is angry or rejecting, or difficulties in worshiping or praying to God.

Many atheists and agnostics who believe they have arrived at their lack of faith by rationally and unemotionally sifting the evidence and concluding that God is not there are actually the victims of an inability to internalize God. Because of emotionally painful experiences in childhood, they have grown up feeling God is not real, present, loving, or powerful. So they conclude—not on the basis of evidence but on the basis of emotion—that God must not exist. Like a baby in a cradle who cannot internalize a parent and feels abandoned when a parent goes away from the cradle, these atheists and agnostics are unable to internalize God. They can't see him, so he must not be there. Maybe they had an experience of God's presence and goodness at some point in their lives, but now he's gone away, it seems, and they can no longer sense him there. It is as if he walked away from their cradle, leaving them feeling alone and insecure.

Many atheists and agnostics, unfortunately, come from Christian homes—homes in which there is a long tradition of church attendance and involvement, of Scripture memorization, of religious activity, of biblically correct doctrine. In other words, these atheists and agnostics were raised in a religious heritage that was rich in the externals of the faith—yet in all too many cases, they were raised in extreme poverty where internalized faith is concerned. They were told what to think about God but never received an experience of how to *feel* toward God. They were given religious forms, so they understood God as a doctrinal concept. But they were not given an opportunity to experience the warm, relational love of God so they could enjoy God as a companion and friend.

God is always nearby, ready to give us a rich, rewarding, eternal life if we commit our lives to him by faith in Jesus Christ. As parents, we need to fill in the holes and deficits of our own experience with God and make sure we are giving our children a rich internal experience of God. The way to do that is to

- affirm your children, show them you enjoy spending time with them, and demonstrate that you are glad to see them
- be physically affectionate with your children; give them a hug, a touch, a pat on the back; show your kids you like to be close to them
- use eye communication when speaking to them *and when listening to them*, to show you are involved and you care
- play with your kids; use *fun* as a bridge to building trust, connection, and relationships
- when you have to discipline your kids, surround your toughness with unconditional love, forgiveness, and a

sense that you want them to live up to their potential; make sure they know that whatever they do, whatever mistakes they make, you are on their side and will never turn your back on them

These may not be the kinds of emotional and spiritual traditions you grew up with as a child. You may have been told at Sunday school that "God is love," only to come home to a house full of anger, grudge bearing, judgment, and retaliation. If so, then you need to replace the defective traditions you were raised in with new and healthy traditions—traditions that will enable your children to experience and internalize God as an affirming, affectionate, loving, forgiving, involved, present, faithful Friend.

A child's early emotional development is one of the greatest determining factors in his spiritual growth. It is the emotional, relational, experiential traditions that surround our children—the way we talk to them, touch them, nurture them, and make them feel loved—that will either enhance or impede their spiritual growth.

New Traditions

DINNER WAS A SMASHING success!

"Hanna dear," warbled Aunt Elma, lifting a forkful, "you must give me your recipe for this bread dressing! Apples and onions—what a wonderful combination!"

"And this turkey!" exclaimed Uncle Albert as he dove into his fourth helping. "So juicy and flavorful. Not dry like last year's—" Glancing at Joanna Brown, he caught himself—a little too late. "I mean, like so many turkeys can be," he finished lamely.

"And the salads!" exulted Cousin Millie. "Pine nuts! I just love pine nuts!"

J. W. and Joanna shifted uncomfortably as the compliments were handed out to Hanna and Scott. Then J. W. rose to his feet, his brow furrowed and a hard look in his eye. "Just a moment, just a moment!" he said loudly, a serious edge to his voice. The chatter around the table died down.

Hanna gulped hard and gave Scott an "uh-oh" look.

"I'd like to say something to this family, if I may," J. W. continued. "Something about tradition. The Brown family was built on tradition. The Brown family survives on tradition. We eat, drink, and breathe tradition. If there's one thing my father, Edward M. Brown, drilled into me, from the time I was as small as little Jenea over there"—he pointed to his eleven-month-old granddaughter, who had just begun walking and was tentatively taking steps while steadying herself on the arm of the sofa—"until he died, it is the importance of tradition. Traditions like education—everyone in the Brown family goes to college and gets an education. Traditions like working hard, being successful, and leaving an inheritance to your children. Traditions like being a good Christian, never missing a Sunday at church, being involved in the church, having a good reputation in the community. Traditions like"—he paused for effect and turned toward Hanna and Scott—"an oven-roasted turkey with oyster dressing."

"Dad—," Hanna began, then stopped when J. W. put his hand up.

"Traditions died hard in the Brown family," he continued. "Now, today we have had a very nontraditional Thanksgiving meal—at least for the Brown family. Today we have seen tradition after tradition broken and disregarded—traditions that have stood since before I was even born! And I have just one thing to say . . ."

As he paused, Hanna held her breath and bit her lip. Scott cringed. The entire family sat in stunned silence around the table.

J. W. leaned forward. "It's about time!"

Still the table was silent. *What* did J. W. say?

A smile broke out across J. W. Brown's face, and he began to clap. "A round of applause," he said, "for my daughter, Hanna, and her husband, Scott, for having the courage to break a few musty old traditions and for making this one of the most memorable Brown family Thanksgivings—ever!"

As the entire table broke out in applause, J. W. leaned over to his daughter and kissed her on the cheek.

"Thank you, Daddy!" she said.

"No, sweetheart," J. W. replied. "Thank *you!*"

Can a Family Be Cursed?

MANY FAMILIES SEEM TO be stuck in unhealthy, unproductive traditions. It may be something as trivial as continuing, year after year, to serve that oyster dressing that nobody likes—or it may be something as serious as an unhealthy religious tradition. Some families pass down a cold and unloving religious spirit, a legalistic pharisaism—which is then transmitted generation by generation, harming each new wave of children it passes through. Other families pass down high expectations of performance: "Our family has always produced pastors and missionaries! What do you mean you want to be an attorney?" Still other families pass down the traditions of sound biblical doctrine, intense church involvement, regular prayer and family devotions—but it is all devoid of family affection, fun, and togetherness.

Family spiritual traditions need to be taken out now and then, dusted off, and examined. Those that are outworn and no longer meaningful should be discarded. Those that are positive and that help our children to grow stronger and deeper in their faith should be strengthened and reinforced.

When I talk to people about their spiritual heritage and family religious traditions, they often raise the issue of "generational curses." They ask, "What about those passages in Exodus in which it says God punishes the sins of the fathers to the third and fourth generations?"

I believe that a generational curse is a consequence of sinful choices made in one generation that echo down to successive generations. A mother who does not deal with an angry, bitter spirit teaches her children to deal with problem situations by blowing up, flying off the handle, and holding grudges—and these coping styles are modeled and passed down to the next generation and the next and the next. A father who does not deal with his preoccupation with lustful thoughts and sexual unfaithfulness can't keep his private thoughts and actions secret from his children forever. They will see the way he looks at other women, or they will find his stash of magazines, or they will pick up unconscious cues and clues—and ultimately, they will likely repeat his sinful pattern in their own lives. Other examples of generationally transmitted sin disorders that I see all the time in my practice include alcoholism, drug abuse, occultism and satanism, suicidal depression, and a tendency toward marital dysfunction and divorce.

Understand, however, that a "generational curse" does not have to doom people to repeat the sins and suffer the consequences of their parents. God is gracious and merciful, and if we commit our ways to him, we can break the cycle of generational sin and avoid passing on our parents' sins to our own children. In Exodus 34:6–7—one of the great passages in which God talks about sin that is punished down to "the third and fourth generation"—God also says that he is a "compassionate and gracious God, slow to anger, abounding in love and faithfulness, maintaining love to thousands, and forgiving wickedness, rebellion and sin."

In a sense, all of us are born under the greatest generational curse of all: the sin of Adam and Eve. We have all inherited a sin nature from the first couple in Eden. But Jesus Christ has made a way of escape for us from the curse of sin, through forgiveness and transformation. Regardless of the sins of your parents, you have a choice as to whether or not you will follow in their footsteps. You have the ability to break the cycle and choose God's way rather than a defective tradition of generational sin.

If you struggle with a particularly difficult and stubborn sin or habit, seek help from a Christian therapist or support group. Make sure that the defective tradition in your family ends with your generation. You don't have to serve sin any more than Hanna had to serve oyster dressing with turkey! You can choose today to serve God—and when you do, you will be making a decision to serve the needs of your children as well.

"Don't Repeat the Mistakes I've Made"

IT WAS A CLEAR, crisp November night. The last carload of relatives pulled away from the curb as J. W., Joanna, Hanna, and Scott—with Jenea in his arms—waved good-bye. Then they all turned and walked back to the house. "What a wonderful Thanksgiving," said Mrs. Brown with a sigh. "I just wish Michael could have been here."

"He was iffy when I talked to him on the phone last night," said Hanna, "but I really thought he was going to be here."

"That's another break with Brown family tradition," J. W. observed, opening the front door and holding it for the others to enter. "Today was the first Thanksgiving we've had without our whole family together."

Inside, Joanna began picking up napkins, paper dessert plates, and Styrofoam cups from the living room. Scott said, "Oh, Joanna, just leave those. I'll clean it up later."

"Goodness," said Mrs. Brown, "it only takes a few moments to—"

"Actually, Joanna," J. W. interrupted, "I'd like everyone to sit down here in the living room for a few minutes. There's something I need to say. Something I need to ... well, to get off my chest."

Glancing at each other but without a word, Joanna, Scott, and Hanna sat down. Scott sat Jenea down on the carpet, but she quickly climbed to her feet and began toddling unsteadily toward her Grandpa Brown.

"Joanna dear, Scott, and Hanna," said J. W., settling into the big, overstuffed recliner, "I have a confession to make." He looked down at the floor, not meeting anyone's eyes. "I confess that I've failed my children—I've failed you spiritually and emotionally. I've failed Michael, and I've failed you too, Hanna."

"Oh no, Daddy," said Hanna. "Don't say that. It's not true."

J. W. held up his hand in the time-honored Brown family gesture that meant, *Hush, I'm speaking now.* "Oh, it's true, all right," he continued. "I've had some talks with Mike over the past few months. He's very angry with me. I've had a hard time understanding why he should feel I've been a poor father to him, and I've been very angry with Mike in return. I sat down with Pastor Knight and told him about Mike—"

Joanna put her hand to her mouth in dismay.

"I know, dear," said J. W., "that you didn't want to talk about this outside the family, but I guess I've reached a point where I care more about Mike and my relationship with him than I care about Brown family pride. Anyway, Pastor Knight referred me to a Christian psychologist, Dr. Knowlton, and I've had three sessions with this counselor, talking about my relationship with Mike."

"Why didn't you tell me," asked Joanna, "that you were seeing a psychologist?"

"I didn't think you'd approve," said J. W. "I felt that what happened with Mike was my fault, so I should be the one to—"

"If I'd have known, I could have gone, too," she replied.

"Mom!" Hanna exclaimed. "You've never wanted to go to anyone for help before. Even when you were going through that awful depression years ago—"

"I know," said Joanna. "But this isn't about me. It's about my son. He's gone away from the Lord. I'd do anything to get him back—even tell my problems to a psychologist."

Hanna's eyes glistened as she turned back to her father. "Go on, Dad. What did you and the doctor talk about?"

"I found out that all these years, I've tried to give Michael a religion when I should have been giving him a relationship. I've spent time building up church programs when I should have been building up my son and my daughter. I probably invested more time and emotional energy as chairman of the building committee than I ever invested in my own children. I've been trying to live up to the Brown family religious traditions—and in the process, I've been destroying the Brown family itself. While trying to preserve and hand down the traditions my father handed down to me, I have overlooked what was most important of all: my children's emotional and spiritual security. It's true that hindsight is twenty-twenty, and it's hard to face your failures thirty years too late. But I want you to know I'm willing to change, even this late in the game. We've broken a lot of traditions today, and I want you to know I'm ready to break more traditions—any traditions—in order to get my son back, in order to bring him back to the Lord."

"What are your plans, Dad?" asked Hanna.

"I don't know yet. I'm still talking with Dr. Knowlton. I'm hoping that Mike might be willing to come in and we could all talk together. Maybe it's not too late to build a bridge of understanding. Maybe it's not too late for me to show Mike how much

I really do love him, even though I've done a terrible job of showing it up until now."

Little Jenea chose that moment to toddle up to J. W.'s knee, as if she wanted to crawl into his lap. J. W. looked down at her, and his eyes instantly filled with tears, which then spilled down his craggy cheeks. He lifted his granddaughter up and hugged her to himself. "Oh, Hanna, Scott, if only Mike could be a little child like this again!" he said, his voice cracking with emotion. "If only I could take him onto my lap and give him a hug—a thousand hugs, all the hugs I should have given him when I was at some stupid church meeting that I don't even remember anymore! Treasure this little one, Hanna. Spend time with her and love her, Scott. Don't repeat the mistakes I've made. Love her and hold her and play with her, just as Jesus would. When you teach her what the Bible says about God, don't forget to *show* her what God is really like. Make that a *new* Brown family tradition, and pass it on to Jenea." He hugged Jenea again, and the little girl ran her hands lovingly over his lined and tear-streaked features.

"We will," said Scott. "Don't worry, J. W., we will."

Without a word, Hanna got up, went to her father's side, and hugged him.

The four of them prayed together that night. They prayed a prayer of love and concern for Michael, their son and brother. And they prayed a prayer of thanksgiving and rededication for little Jenea. They prayed believing that God would act in the lives of these two special family members—one who had gone away from the faith, and another who was too young to comprehend their prayers. They prayed hoping and believing—but not knowing what the future would hold.

FIVE

The Spiritual Growth Process

I'M GLAD YOU DECIDED to come, Michael," said Dr. Knowlton.
"Yeah, well, I guess it doesn't hurt to talk," Michael responded with a shrug.

"I really appreciate it, Son," said J. W.

"I'd like to open with a word of prayer," said Dr. Knowlton. Michael did not object.

"Lord," began the psychologist, "we're grateful that we can all be here and that you are here with us. We ask you to lead us into all truth, because even though the truth can be painful, only the truth can set us free. Give us the ability to truly hear and understand each other as we open ourselves to each other and to you. In the name of Jesus, amen."

"I have to tell you, right from the get-go," Michael said quickly, "that I don't believe in prayer. I don't believe in God."

"No one requires you to," said the doctor. "We're just here to talk and create some understanding—and some healing, if possible."

"I'm willing to *listen*," said Michael. "As far as *talking*—well, I don't know what I would have to say."

"That's fair enough," said Dr. Knowlton. "I believe your father has something he wants to say."

Michael turned a hard glance toward his dad. "Oh? What's that, Dad?" The tone of Michael's voice was a ringing accusation, as if he expected nothing from his father but excuses.

"I wanted to say," J. W. began, speaking slowly and softly, looking down at his shoes, "that I'm sorry. I was never there for you when you needed me. I wasn't there pulling for you at your ball games. I never helped you with your homework. I never took you fishing or to a big-league game. If I tucked you into bed at night, it was usually after you were asleep. I stuffed your head with Bible verses and took you to Sunday school and youth group two, three times a week, but I don't remember that we ever just sat on the front porch on a summer night, looking at the stars and talking about the universe God had made. I don't remember ever talking to you about the meaning of life, or how to be a man. All those years while you were growing up I spent doing religious things but never doing the spiritual thing. The years while you were growing up are all gone now, and neither you nor I will ever get them back."

Michael sat in stunned silence, unable to speak.

J. W.'s head slowly raised up, and his red-rimmed eyes looked despairingly, almost pleadingly, into Michael's eyes. "I'd give anything to get those years back, Michael. The thing is ... I love you, Son."

Psychology and Faith

IN ORDER TO UNDERSTAND the process of spiritual growth, we need to examine the delicate relationship between psychology—the study of human thinking, feeling, and behavior—and theology, the study of God. Historically, the field of psychology has had a somewhat rocky relationship with Christianity. In recent years, the field of "pop psychology" has been the target of harsh (and often well-deserved) attacks by Christian authors and speakers. The concern among many in the Christian community is that psychology attempts to seduce people into relying on human understanding rather than God's revealed Word. Some even view psychology as a substitute for spirituality and thus a threat to spirituality.

In recent years, however, noted Christian psychologists and psychiatrists such as Dr. James Dobson, Dr. Frank Minirth, Dr. Paul Meier, Dr. Bruce Narramore, and others have been very effective in using biblically based principles along with psychological and medical insight to dramatically help people with emotional and mental problems, relational problems, addictions, spiritual problems, and related issues. As a result, many Christians who were once closed-minded or antagonistic toward psychology are finding that some of the insights and discoveries of this field are enabling Christians to live richer, healthier lives and enabling the church to better carry out its mission in the world. For example, the psychological research conducted by Jean Piaget into the stages of a child's mental development has been extremely valuable in enabling Christian educators to develop age-appropriate Sunday school curriculum.

I understand the antipsychology feelings of many Christians, because I once shared those feelings. I entered seminary in 1984 with the intention of becoming a pastoral counselor, not a psychologist. One Tuesday morning at 10:00 A.M., I walked into a seminary class that was soon to change my thinking—and my life. It was a class I was taking for my Christian counseling degree. Bible in hand, I sat down expecting a course in how to counsel out of the Bible. But as the professor began his first lecture, I was disappointed.

"You will find, as you begin counseling people," he said, "that not every problem a counselee presents to you is a spiritual problem. That person may not need more prayer, more Scripture, or more faith. Let's say a pastor comes to you, a Christian counselor, and says, 'I'm burned out. I can't keep up with the demands of the ministry anymore.' What would you tell him? That he needs more faith? That he's not committed enough? That he doesn't have it as bad as Moses or some other Bible character? It may well be that the insight he needs is that he is burned out because of a tendency to be a 'people pleaser.' He may need to hear that if he doesn't adopt more realistic expectations of himself, he will end up experiencing a complete mental and emotional breakdown, resulting in his resignation from the ministry. These are psychological, not biblical, insights—but of course, these psychological insights should be reinforced with biblical truth, such as the facts that the Lord's yoke is easy and his burden is light, that we should not heap higher expectations on ourselves than God himself places on us, and that Jesus didn't minister twenty-four hours a day, either. But the point is that if we apply *only* biblical insights and ignore the truths we have learned from the field of psychology, we would not be helping this man, his ministry, his congregation, or the cause of Jesus Christ."

Now, I confess that as I listened to those words, I bristled inside. I was a naive, judgmental seminary student with all the pride and arrogance of youth. I was ready to get up and walk out of that class rather than listen to any more of this heresy! But for some reason, I stayed. I listened, mentally rebelling against what I was hearing.

And then a moment came when understanding just seemed to break through my resistance and my will. I experienced one of those "Aha!" moments, when everything just seemed to click into place, snap into focus, and suddenly make sense. Instantly it hit me that while everything contained in the Bible is true, not everything that is true is in the Bible. But more importantly, I realized that the concept this professor was trying to impart to me dovetailed perfectly with the Bible's view of human beings and human nature. Something in this professor's lecture enabled me to grasp a biblical truth that I had never before fully grasped in my undergraduate courses—the truth that human beings are made of three dimensions or components. It is the truth contained in 1 Thessalonians 5:23: "May God himself, the God of peace, sanctify you through and through. May your whole spirit, soul and body be kept blameless at the coming of our Lord Jesus Christ." That is what we are as human beings: a *body*, a *soul*, and a *spirit*, each distinct, yet all bound together and interconnected. For our purposes, the focus will remain primarily on the soul and the spirit.

The Greek word for soul is *psyche*, a word with various meanings in the New Testament but usually used in reference to the self. The soul, or *psyche*, is functionally distinct from both the body and the

Flesh - Spirit Link

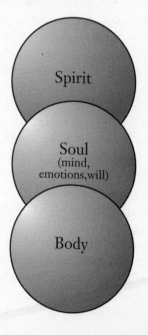

spirit. With the body, an individual has contact with the physical world, the world of the senses. With the spirit, an individual reaches toward and makes contact with the spiritual world, the world of God and eternity. Between the body and the spirit lives the soul, or *psyche*, with its psychological functions—the mind, the emotions, and the will. Psychology, then, is the study of the human soul.

The Bible frequently refers to three basic functions of the soul. For example, in Job 6:7, reference is made to the will, which is the ability of the soul to make choices. Proverbs 19:2 refers to the intellectual, or knowing, aspect of the soul—the mind. Finally, Song of Songs 1:7 refers to the emotional function of the soul.

People often confuse the human soul with the human spirit. The spirit, however, differs from the soul and is the supernatural dimension of a human being, created in that human being at conception. The human spirit is not to be confused with the Holy Spirit of God, received by Christians at the time of conversion.

Just as there are three functions to the soul (mind, emotions, and will), there are three basic functions of the spirit. First, the spirit is our mechanism for knowing God. Second, the spirit is the seat of the human conscience. Third, after the Holy Spirit comes to take residence within the human spirit, the Spirit provides supernatural perception and insight, independent of mental reasoning. We see this aspect of the spirit at work in Mark 2:8, which says that "Jesus knew in his spirit" what a group of men "were thinking in their hearts"—in other words, Jesus was exercising a perceiving function of his spirit, while these other men were exercising a mental function of their souls.

Over the years, I've seen again and again that the provable insights and principles of psychology mesh seamlessly with the revealed insights and principles of God's Word. Psychological concepts or theories that violate God's Word invariably end up being discarded or revised after time and experience prove them wrong or inadequate. In many cases, psychology describes processes, outcomes, and disorders, while the Bible gives us the underlying reasons for those processes, outcomes, and disorders.

I know beyond any doubt that everything in the Bible is true. But I also know that there is much that is true that is not found in the Bible. You do not turn to the Bible to learn how to change the oil in your car or how to operate your computer. For that kind of truth, you consult a car manual or a computer manual. In a similar way, if you want to know how to treat certain emotional disorders, you turn to the field of psychology; at the same time, however, the Bible can explain the sin, the lack of faith and hope, or the lack of spiritual connection to God that underlies or amplifies many psychological problems. By bringing both the insights of psychology and the insights of the Bible to bear on a problem, we can do a more thorough job of addressing and solving the problem and bringing spiritual and emotional health to the client.

Psychology should never be used as a substitute for faith or biblical insight—only as a supplement to it. If the principles of psychology ever come into conflict with the principles of the Bible, it is the principles of psychology that must give way, and the principles of the Bible that must be applied. But kept in proper perspective, psychological principles about human nature and human development can be useful in removing roadblocks to the faith development of your child so that he can enjoy a richer lifelong experience of relationship with God.

Faith and the Context of Relationships

SPIRITUAL GROWTH DOES NOT occur in a vacuum but occurs within a context of relationships. When a child is born, God gives that child the potential and the drive, or motivation, to grow in five areas: physical, mental, relational, emotional, and spiritual. In addition, God has ordained parents to guide this growth within each child, from birth to adulthood. In order for children to fully mature, they must have parents or primary caregivers who are themselves mature in these five areas. The child of emotionally stunted parents tends to become handicapped emotionally; the child of spiritually stunted parents tends to be spiritually stunted.

Spiritual growth should occur in concert with all other areas of individual growth—physical, mental, emotional, and relational. Each area of growth is linked to and influenced by every other area of growth. One of the most important factors affecting the growth of your child's spirituality is your child's relational development. Spiritual growth takes place within the context of personal family relationships, and the most powerful and effective thing you can do to encourage and enhance your child's faith is to build a close, warm, bonded relationship with your child.

The God-given instincts within a child provide the energy and drive necessary for total emotional growth as well as for growth in the other domains—mental, relational, physical, and spiritual. Through the experience of an intimate personal relationship between a child and his parents, these instinctive inner drives are either satisfied or frustrated. For example, if a child naturally looks for attention from his parents by doing something to be noticed but is ignored or told by his parents to "get lost," then his natural growth drive has been stifled. The child will feel frustrated with himself, with his primary caregivers, and with life in general. More important, the child does not understand what is happening and cannot adequately communicate his needs. But if the child receives the attention he desires, his growth drive is satisfied and he feels peace about himself, his primary caregivers, and his life.

So relationships exert a powerful influence over the spiritual well-being of a child—for good or for ill. Painful or unhealthy relational experiences can produce distortions and disorders in a child's spiritual being. I call this "spiritual contamination." Though none of us can achieve complete spiritual purity in this life, we can imagine a spiritually pure system in theory.

Spiritually Pure System

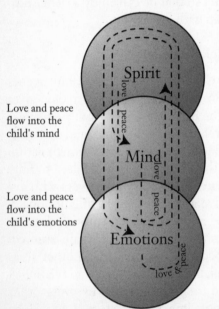

Love and peace flow into the child's mind

Love and peace flow into the child's emotions

The diagram on page 80 represents a child, who we will call Carrie, who is presently experiencing a life filled with love and peace as received from the Spirit.

We experience an increase or decrease in the purity of our spiritual experience according to various factors in our lives—factors that are rooted in the human soul. Painful emotions, sinful choices, guilt and shame, broken relationships, and the poisonous residue of neglect or abuse can *affect* and *infect* the human spirit, producing contamination. This contamination tends to diminish our ability to experience the joy, peace, presence, and insight of the Holy Spirit alongside our own spirit. Understand that it is only our human spiritual experience that can ever be diminished, not the Holy Spirit within us; this fruit always remains untainted.

A spiritually contaminated system is diagrammed below.

Consider this hypothetical scenario using our child named Carrie. In this diagram, five-year-old Carrie started her morning

Spiritually Contaminated System

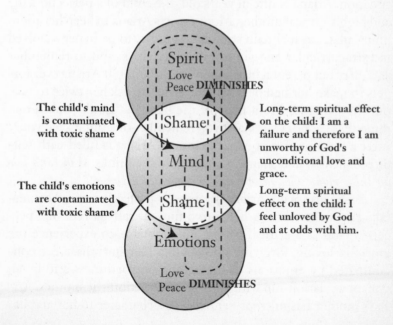

off with a relatively pure system. As she sat at the breakfast table, she was feeling loved and at peace with her small world. It was at this point that she spilled the milk all over the table and her father's lap. Her father rose from the table, enraged, and shouted, "Are you stupid or something? What in the world are you trying to do, pouring milk all over me!" As feelings of shame flow from her father's words into her fragile and sensitive emotions, the peace and love Carrie had previously experienced diminishes considerably. Consider the long-term spiritual effects that shame can cause to Carrrie's present and future relationships to her *heavenly* father.

Spiritual contamination is much like a physical disease. It makes us feel spiritually weak and sick. It desensitizes us to the power and influence of the Holy Spirit in our lives. Spiritual contamination leaves us spiritually crippled—and even spiritually paralyzed. It renders us more vulnerable to potential attacks from Satan. For this very reason, the New Testament encourages us to "purify ourselves from everything that contaminates body and spirit" (2 Cor. 7:1).

Here's how spiritual contamination takes place in a real-life situation: Ariana is fifteen years old, the child of a perfectionistic and highly critical mother. Mom expects Ariana to keep her room immaculate, to maintain straight-A grades, to be hyper-involved in extracurricular and youth group activities, and to remember and carry out parental instructions to the letter. If Ariana ever forgets to make her bed or if Mom ever has to ask her twice to take out the garbage, Mom flies off the handle: "Can't you do one thing that I ask of you? Can't you remember one thing I tell you?" After a few minutes of Mom's ranting, Ariana is filled with self-directed anger and shame. *I'm so stupid!* she thinks. *Why can't I do anything right? God must really be displeased with me.*

As she grows up, Ariana is intensely perfectionistic. Any mistake she makes throws her into a funk of self-hatred. She perceives God as a critical parent and is unable to experience the gracious, loving, forgiving side of God. Her spirit has been contaminated by emotions of shame and unworthiness and by an unhappy relationship with an overly perfectionistic mother. Ariana's mother has misrepresented God's character to her and has made it difficult for her to experience the level of peace and one-ness with God that God himself intended her to have. In order to experience a rich, healthy relationship with God—the abundant joy that Jesus said he came to bring us—Ariana will need to have her spirit purified.

Spiritual Decontamination

I CALL IT "SPIRITUAL decontamination"—a process of removing distortions, impurities, and obstacles from our image of God, and our relationship with God. To be spiritually decontaminated means that we change false beliefs about God and false emotions toward God. We replace those distorted thoughts and feelings with God's truth about himself, as revealed in the Bible. The illustration on the next page graphically represents the process.

Thinking back to five-year-old Carrie's dilemma, let's take her through the decontamination process. In this diagram, stage one, contamination, reflects how the love and peace Carrie experienced prior to spilling the milk has been replaced by toxic shame (shame that says, "I am bad and unworthy"). Stage two, decontamination, reflects the inner spirit of love and peace being restored in this wounded child. This healing process in Carrie's situation is a result of her mother's willingness to minister to her with truth shortly after the crisis. When her father left for work, Carrie's mother gently held her, saying, "Everything will be okay. Mommy loves you, God loves you, and Daddy still loves you too, even though he got angry. You are a good girl."

The third stage, purification, is evidence that Carrie has accepted as truth what her mother said to her and has internalized it. This opens the door for the love and peace in Carrie's small world to return.

Once decontamination takes place, a clear connection between the Spirit of God and the human spirit can take place. We experience fellowship with God, just as he intended us to. We experience the abundant life and the joy of knowing God—not as a theological concept but as a close Friend, a caring and accepting heavenly Parent.

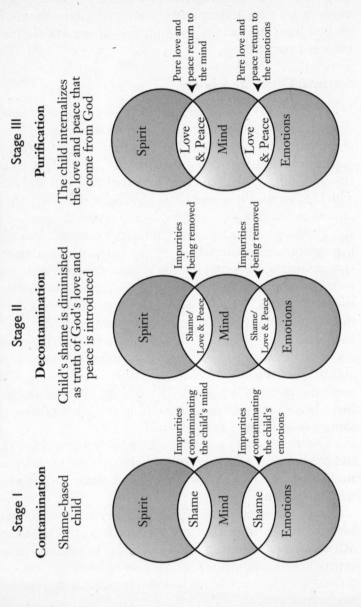

Spiritually Decontaminated System

Stage I
Contamination
Shame-based child

Stage II
Decontamination
Child's shame is diminished as truth of God's love and peace is introduced

Stage III
Purification
The child internalizes the love and peace that come from God

Impurities contaminating the child's mind

Impurities contaminating the child's emotions

Impurities being removed

Impurities being removed

Pure love and peace return to the mind

Pure love and peace return to the emotions

Spirit — Shame — Mind — Shame — Emotions

Spirit — Shame/Love & Peace — Mind — Shame/Love & Peace — Emotions

Spirit — Love & Peace — Mind — Love & Peace — Emotions

It is important to understand that spiritual contamination can take place in various ways. Our parents and other significant people in our lives can contaminate us from without, by means of poor modeling of God's character, by communicating to us distorted information about God, or by wounding us emotionally. We can also contaminate ourselves spiritually from within, by sinning against God and heaping guilt, shame, and a sense of unworthiness upon ourselves. Furthermore, even when the contamination comes from without—say, because of poor parental modeling or outright abuse—we often maintain and even magnify the contamination from within, by holding on to impure, sinful, or bitter emotions. It is certainly unhealthy to believe these feelings and to trust them while ignoring the truth about ourselves that God wants us to know: that he stands ready to forgive us and restore us, no matter what we have done, no matter what someone else may have done to us. It is not God's will that we hold on to shame and anger. He wants us to experience a pure spirit in constant fellowship and life-giving communion with his Holy Spirit.

When a child demonstrates evidence of spiritual contamination, our task as parents (or stepparents or grandparents or Sunday school teachers or neighbors or whatever) is to help that child replace contaminated thoughts about God with accurate thoughts about God. We do this not so much by educating the child in biblically correct doctrine but by finding ways to take emotions of loneliness, depression, worry, anxiety, bitterness, isolation, and shame in that child and replace them with a sense of love, affirmation, security, and worth. This is not something that happens easily or instantaneously in the life of a child—or an adult. Negative thinking must gradually be repatterned. Negative experiences must be replaced with positive experiences. Negative feelings must be purged by feelings of love, joy, and forgiveness.

The entire process of spiritual decontamination may take years—or even a lifetime. But as you seek ways to love that child with the love of Jesus Christ, as you gradually build that child's sense of security, and as you surround and baptize that child with your prayers, God will break through the barriers in that child's life. Soon a maximum therapeutic dose of the Holy Spirit will begin flowing through that child as the spiritual contamination in his system begins to break down. The result will be a gradually increasing demonstration of such qualities as love, joy, peace, patience, kindness, goodness, faithfulness, gentleness, and self-control—qualities that Galatians 5:22–23 calls the fruit of the Spirit.

But don't expect overnight change. The spiritual decontamination process usually takes time—and patience. It does not happen overnight.

"A Little Late ..."

THE WORDS HUNG IN the air as if frozen in time: "I'd give anything to get those years back, Michael. The thing is ... I love you, Son."

A mixture of conflicting emotions played across Michael's face. He seemed poised on the brink of a decision. His features seemed to soften for a moment. His eyes, so full of anger just moments before, now seemed to melt with something sad and tender—compassion perhaps, or pity. But it was only a brief flicker. Then the hardness and the coldness descended over Michael's face once again, like a mask of steel.

"Don't you think," Michael said at last, "it's a little late for that, Dad?"

J. W.'s chin sank onto his chest. "Yes," he admitted miserably. "I suppose it is."

Is IT TOO LATE for J. W. and his son, Michael? Perhaps not.

SIX

The Four Dimensions of Spiritual Growth

IT WAS THE DAY before Jenea's second birthday. Last year, Hanna had bought a bakery cake. This year, no matter how busy and hectic things were, Hanna had determined to make Jenea a birthday cake from scratch. It had been more of a chore than she expected, however, and by the time she finally got the two cake pans into the oven and turned around to look at her kitchen, she was dismayed to see the mess that had to be cleaned up.

Well, at least Jenea was still asleep. Hanna would have time to get the kitchen clean before her little two-year-old terror was up from her nap, raising havoc from one end of the house to the other.

Hanna cleaned up the eggshells, the spilled sugar and flour, and put away the tins of baking powder and cream of tartar. She closed her well-worn copy of *Joy of Cooking*, with its cracked spine and Crisco-stained pages—and was about to put it on the shelf with her other cookbooks, when she thought of Aunt Elma, who had given that cookbook to her as a high school graduation present and who had gone to be with the Lord just a couple months ago.

Just then she heard Jenea calling for her. "Momma! Momma! Jenea get up now, Momma!"

"Yes, sweetheart," Hanna replied, heading for Jenea's bedroom, "you can get up now. Did you have a nice nap?" She found Jenea leaning on the side rail that prevented her from rolling out of bed while she slept. The toddler could have crawled around that rail and got out of bed anytime she wanted to—but she didn't know that. Sweetly, obediently, she always awaited her mother's permission before officially ending her nap and getting out of bed.

Hanna reached down and swept the child up in her arms. "You know what Mommy was doing while you were taking a nap?"

Jenea reached up and stroked her mother's face with both hands. "What Mommy doing?"

"I was making a birthday cake for Jenea! You're going to be two years old tomorrow. And we're going to have Grandma and Grandpa Brown and Uncle Mike over here, and you're going to get presents and eat cake! Won't that be fun?"

Jenea clapped her hands. "Yaaaaayyyyyy!"

In that peaceful, happy moment, neither Jenea nor her mother had any inkling as to what the next half hour would bring.

———

SPIRITUAL GROWTH DOES NOT take place haphazardly. It develops in an orderly fashion, through an identifiable set of developmental stages. Humans are complex beings, and we can view the development of an individual through a variety of "filters" or "dimensions." Each dimension is intimately linked with, is affected by, and exerts influence over every other. The four most important dimensions, which we will examine in this chapter, are

1. faith development
2. personality (emotional) development
3. cognitive (mental) development
4. moral development

The Stages of Faith Development

IN 1980 JAMES FOWLER, then a Harvard-trained theologian with a background in developmental psychology, published a book called *Stages of Faith*, the result of ten years of research on faith development in human beings. Fowler's work has proven invaluable to child development specialists, Christian educators, and Sunday school curriculum publishers. Fowler was the first researcher to map the four identifiable stages of faith development.

Primal faith. The first stage of faith development takes place in prenatal time and infancy. The mother's frame of mind during pregnancy (and the attitudes, feelings, and behavior of those closest to her) have an impact on the basic formation of the child's mental, emotional, and spiritual being.

Intuitive projective faith. This stage of faith begins about the time a child learns to speak and use language, and continues through about kindergarten age. It is a stage in which the child's imagination, perceptions, and feelings govern his view of the world. Instead of receiving information from the world and forming impressions of reality, the child intuitively forms impressions and projects those impressions onto his understanding of the world. The child is strongly influenced by the stories and images of faith we provide. These stories affirm important truths like the sovereignty of God and the love of Jesus Christ. The child will receive these stories with interest and appreciation but may not be able to repeat them back to you with a full sense of what these stories mean.

Mythical literal faith. Children commonly move through this stage during their elementary school years. At this stage, children are better able to reason. They are able to sort out the real from the unreal and are able to use stories and content from the Bible to formulate spiritual concepts and interpret spiritual experiences. The child seeks definite answers and explanations, such as are found in myths, and seeks to apply those answers and explanations to life in a literal, practical way. Children in this stage are able to communicate their spiritual concepts to others.

Synthetic conventional faith. Though the word *synthetic* is often used in the sense of something artificial, here it is used in the sense of something that is synthesized, made up of two or more components. At this stage, the child begins to form his own story out of components from the Bible, his religious instruction, and his own experience. He struggles to find continuity between the self he has been, the self he seems to be, and the self he will become. He relates the stories of the Bible to his own story, to his past and present experiences, and to his hopes and fears about the future. This stage begins in adolescence and continues toward young adulthood, as the child seeks to find personal meaning in the Bible and in the religious instruction he receives.

These stages of faith will vary from child to child, from situation to situation. But they provide one way of delineating the pattern of a child's growth in the ability to receive, grasp, and assimilate stories and information from God's Word.[1]

The "Aminals" and the "Wainbow"

"WHAT STORY WOULD YOU like to read?" asked Hanna, taking the children's Bible-story book down from the shelf.

"Cake now!" Jenea responded, tugging at her mother's blouse.

"No-no!" laughed Hanna, imitating her daughter's phrasing. "Cake tomorrow. Read now."

"Cake now!" Jenea insisted loudly.

"I'm going to read you a story now, Jenea. What story would you like?"

"Moses takes the aminals."

"Moses takes the animals?" asked Hanna, bewildered. She sat down in the rocking chair, pulled Jenea into her lap, and began flipping through the storybook, looking for the story in which "Moses takes the aminals." She found a picture of Moses throwing down his rod, and another picture in which the rod turns into a snake. "You mean this story?" asked Hanna.

"No! Not that Moses! Moses takes the aminals! On the water!"

Hanna turned back a few pages, to where the baby Moses was in a basket on the river, floating among the bulrushes. "You mean this one?"

"No! No! No! Not that Moses! Moses takes the aminals on the water to see the wainbow!"

"Oh!" Hanna responded, suddenly realizing what her daughter wanted. "You don't mean Moses. You mean Noah and the ark."

"I mean this Moses," said Jenea, grabbing the book and flipping back a few more pages until she found a story called "The First Rainbow" and a picture of Noah building his boat. She began telling the story from the pictures, turning pages as she went. "This is Moses and ... and ... and ... and ... and he took all the elephants and aminals and monkeys on the ship on the water and

... and ... and ... and it wained and wained on the water and ... and ... and ... and he took the birds and the aminals to see the wainbow and the wainbow was pretty and The End."

"Well, that was a very nice story, Jenea."

"Uh-huh. Let's wead it again."

The Foundations of Faith Development

IN ORDER TO DEVELOP in a healthy way, a child's faith should be built on a foundation of five ingredients—trust, imagination, ritualization, culture, and internalization. Let's examine each of these crucial ingredients in turn.

Trust

In my own study, I have read dozens of experts in the field of faith development—experts such as Jack R. Gib, Juanita Hart, John J. Gleason, Iris V. Cully, Eric Erickson, and Lucy Bregman—and the one common thread that runs through all of their conclusions is the word *trust*. In fact, you could define *faith* as "trust in the existence, character, truth, power, and love of God." We know that children whose capacity for trust is diminished in childhood become almost invariably adults who have a hard time trusting other people—and trusting God. When parents break promises, betray confidences, behave in unpredictable ways, or commit acts of abuse, a child's capacity for trust is damaged. A child with an untrustworthy earthly parent becomes wary and untrusting in his relationship with the heavenly Parent, God himself.

Everything God provides for us—love, mercy, forgiveness, power, and answered prayer—must be appropriated through faith. In the original Greek language of the Bible, the noun *faith* (*pistis*) and the verb *to trust* (*pisteuo*) are forms of the same word. In theological terms, faith is a necessary requirement for a life of godliness. In psychological terms, trust is a necessary requirement for a life of wholeness and good mental-emotional health. The ability to trust others is one of the foundations in the development of all healthy human personality.

In his landmark book *Childhood and Society*, child development researcher Eric Erickson shows that the first crisis of childhood, which must be resolved in the first year and a half of life, is the crisis of "trust versus mistrust." This is the foundation for all other developments of personality. A child who learns to trust his primary caregivers, who learns to rely upon the love and care of parents, is a child with an intact capacity for trusting God. This is not to say that such a child will automatically develop faith in God—there is more to the faith development process than the mere capacity for trust. Nor is this to say that a child of abusive or otherwise untrustworthy parents cannot develop faith in God—only that such a child will have greater emotional obstacles to overcome. God is gracious and often performs miracles of healing and intervention in lives that have been horribly wounded by bad parenting or other painful experiences.

As Christian parents, however, we want to give our children's faith every possible opportunity to develop and grow. That means we must do everything we can to enhance our children's capacity for trust. We do this, says Erickson, by meeting the needs of our children, by tenderly holding and touching them, by smiling and talking to them, by building what he calls "a trust account" in their lives.[2]

As Lucy Bregman notes in her book *Through the Landscape of Faith*,

> The infant's experience of mutuality between itself and its mother fosters an abiding sense of trust and loyalty that endures throughout life. This infantile trust also provides an experiential grounding for much religious symbolism of loving intimacy.[3]

In other words, a child's earliest experiences of relying on his caretakers for physical and emotional nurturing provide the foundation for a later faith-based intimate relationship with his unseen heavenly Father. This early process is best described as an *experiential faith*—a faith that is not taught by words but "caught" by experience.

Imagination

Studies indicate that imagination is present in the earliest stages of infancy. Imagination is our innate, God-given ability to link our inner world of thinking with our inner world of feeling. Through the imagination, we can undergo emotions and impressions without experiencing actual events. We can sense what it would be like to walk with Jesus, to be a child on his knee, to be a Roman soldier at the foot of the cross, to be a disciple at the empty tomb.

In an article on faith development, David J. Loomis writes,

> Imagination is the cognitive facility that mediates a person's relationship with God. Through imagination the Scriptures reach out to grip us with their baffling mysteries. God's Word made flesh enters our hearts through the filter of imagination.[4]

While God has given us a capacity for imagination at an early age, it is a highly fragile gift. Imagination must be supported and nurtured so that our children can perceive God and his love to be within the realm of possibility.

Ritualization

A third foundation of faith development is ritualization. We all become aware of ourselves and our place in the world through everyday rituals: being fed, tended, cleansed, and put to bed on a regular, ritualized basis. As early as two to six months of age, infants are able to learn to relate to and interact with caregivers through ritualized patterns of behavior and familiarity.

An example of ritualization is the pattern of games played between parent and child—games of peekaboo or tickle or making faces that are played and replayed on a regular basis and enable a child to experience the parent as a source of pleasure, fun, affirmation, and mutual enjoyment. As the child matures, he observes other rituals in the family that point to the presence of God within the family—nightly prayer and devotions or prayer at the dinner table. Other ritualized, symbolic gestures of faith—heads bowed at prayer, or the exchange of gifts at Christmas—help to shape the spiritual perceptions of a child. The child learns through these rituals that God is an unseen member of the family.

Culture

The fourth foundation of early faith development is culture—the total social environment a child experiences from birth onward. Culture has an impact upon the child's sense of self, of others, and of God. Identity as a member of God's family is communicated through various events in everyday living. Children who are part of a faith community are enriched as they journey deeper into the experience of knowing God.

Internalization

We discussed internalization in chapter 4. Whereas most of the ways we impart the Christian faith to our children tend to be through external means—preaching, teaching, storytelling, and other forms of conveying information—the most effective way to impart the Christian faith is through internal means such as emotional experiences. Our ultimate goal is not merely to impart Christian data to our children but to enable them to experience the living reality of God's loving presence.

In psychology, the term *internalize* refers to one's ability to retain the feeling of an object within oneself, even after the object is removed. For example, when a baby cries, you pick him up, hold him, speak soothingly, and meet his needs; soon the crying ceases. During this process, the baby perceives you as a warm and nurturing object and absorbs sensations from you—your touch, voice, fragrance, and eye communication. These sensations translate into feelings of warmth and security that the child internalizes, or takes within himself. You can then put the baby back in his cradle and walk away. He will continue to be happy and quiet for a while, because he has internalized you. He keeps the emotional sensation of his experience of you within himself. If he could not internalize his parents in this way, he could not emotionally survive the developmental stage of infancy—he would be screaming all the time!

Many people have trouble internalizing God as a source of security and nurturing. They cannot emotionally trust God; they cannot sense his presence. Sound doctrines and biblically correct teaching may give us guidance for living our lives, but they don't help us internalize God. Internalization is something that happens on an emotional and experiential level, not on a cognitive or informational level.

If we can't sense God's presence, it is certainly not because God is not there. Instead, it may well be that we are unable to adequately internalize him. God is always nearby, ready to give us a rich, rewarding, eternal life if we commit our lives to him by faith in Jesus Christ.

Horror in the Breakfast Nook

HANNA HAD JUST FINISHED reading the story of "Moses takes the aminals" when the oven buzzer sounded, announcing that the cake was ready to come out of the oven. She set Jenea down on the floor, got out of the rocker, and headed for the kitchen. Jenea followed her. Once in the kitchen, Hanna warned, "Stay back! Hot! Hot!" Then she opened the oven and checked both halves of the cake, inserting and withdrawing a toothpick. Seeing that they were done, Hanna took the pans out of the oven and set them on trivets on the table in the breakfast nook.

"Cake now! Cake now!" begged Jenea.

"No, honey. The cake's not ready to eat yet. Very hot! We'll eat cake tomorrow."

But what does a two-year-old know about "tomorrow"? Jenea continued to insist, "Cake now! Cake now!"

Hanna sighed. "Come with me, sweetheart. I'll get you a Hostess cupcake."

"Cake! Cake! Yaaaaayyyyyy!"

Hanna led Jenea to the pantry and began rummaging around among the cereal boxes and potato chip bags and microwave popcorn packages, in search of Hostess cupcakes. The phone rang. "Just a moment, sweetie," said Hanna, leaving the pantry door open. As her mother left to answer the phone, Jenea found some interesting things to look at and handle on a lower shelf—two-liter bottles of soda pop and cans of tomato juice.

Lifting the receiver to her ear, Hanna said, "Hello?"

"Hello," said a tinny voice in the phone. "This is an automated message. Please don't hang up. We have important news for people sixty-five and older, concerning an important insurance plan that picks up where Medicare leaves off—"

Mildly annoyed, Hanna hung up the phone, then peered around the pantry door to check on Jenea.

Jenea was gone. Where could she have run off to so fast? Then, from the direction of the breakfast nook, Hanna heard a tiny laughing, innocent voice: "Cake now! Cake now!"

"Oh, no! Jenea, don't touch!" cried Hanna, whirling in the direction of the breakfast nook—

Too late.

As if in slow motion, she watched in horror as Jenea grasped the end of the tablecloth and pulled. Hanna saw the oven-hot cake pans moving across the table, directly toward her little girl. She even saw little wisps of steam curling up from the pans as Jenea dragged them inexorably toward the edge of the table. Hanna tried to move, but though time seemed to slow down, so did her arms and legs. There was simply no way she could reach Jenea in time.

The cake pans jutted over the edge of the table, over Jenea's upturned face. They tottered. They fell.

Hanna screamed.

Then Jenea screamed.

The Stages of Personality (Emotional) Development

ERIC ERICKSON HAS OUTLINED the personality and emotional growth stages in a way that gives us "handles" to assess the spiritual progress of our children at various ages and stages. Though Erickson did not approach this subject from a theological or spiritual point of view, he did use language that has theological as well as psychological significance: trust, faith, identity. These words are easily translated into religious or spiritual growth categories. By understanding how our children progress at each stage of personality and emotional development, we can better understand and meet their psychological and spiritual needs. As a result, we will be better able to give our children the appropriate spiritual education and spiritual experiences for each stage they encounter.

Erickson defines each developmental stage as a "psychosocial crisis," a kind of passage or turning point that is triggered by a combination of the child's own developmental readiness, coupled with changes or pressures brought on by the child's environment or society. Each person goes through a series of life stages; every stage begins when a capacity first appears, and lasts until the capacity is so well established and integrated that the next stage can safely be initiated. At the end of each stage, a crisis emerges, and the individual makes an unconscious decision either to go forward or to remain in the same stage. The process could be viewed as a "ladder of accomplishment," and with each crisis that is successfully negotiated, the individual moves another rung up that ladder. These stages of development are not disorderly. Each stage carries the individual on to the next stage.

Erickson's eight stages of personality (emotional) development follow.

Infancy Stage: Birth to Fifteen Months Old (Task: Trust)

During the infancy stage, the child is totally dependent upon his parents (primarily mom) for physical and emotional care. During this stage, the child must feel loved and secure, and must be able to trust his primary caretakers in a growing way.

Toddler Stage: Fifteen Months to Three Years Old (Task: Autonomy)

The crucial task of the toddler stage is the development of a sense of autonomy and independence as a separate individual. At this stage, self-esteem and the ability to control needs, desires, and feelings are developed. In a healthy family system, the child also learns to develop a positive attitude toward those who are in authority over him.

Preschool Stage: Three to Six Years Old (Task: Initiative)

This is the critical time for the child to begin assuming personal responsibility for coping with his world. This occurs because of his God-given drive for initiative, or positive motivation. Normally, the child will be enthusiastic and happy about learning. He continues the process, begun in the toddler stage, of learning by physically exploring his environment.

Latency Stage: Six to Twelve Years Old (Task: Industry)

The elementary school years are characterized by industry and activity resulting from a combination of the child's continued motivation for learning and an inborn drive for increasing independence. At this stage, the concepts of self-confidence, sexual identity, social identity, and family identity are formed. Self-discipline begins to solidify, and the child normally begins to develop internal control, to carry out responsibilities, and to receive feedback from his conscience.

Adolescent Stage: Twelve to Twenty-one Years Old (Task: Identity)

This stage is the most crucial stage for developing a sense of identity. The adolescent actively searches for his final, complete identity—who he is, his purpose in life, the meaning of life, his place in the world. He must come to accept himself as a distinct, worthwhile person. This adolescent searching is a universal response to the inborn drives given by the Creator.

Young Adult Stage: Twenty-two to Thirty-five Years Old (Task: Intimacy)

The critical task of young adulthood is to experience authentic intimacy—the fulfillment of our human capacity for emotional interchange. Young adults need to learn both to give and to receive on an emotional level, without fear of hurting others or being hurt. Accordingly, this is the period when individuals generally achieve the task of committing themselves to the long-term relationship of marriage.

Middle Adult Stage: Thirty-five to Fifty-five Years Old (Task: Generativity)

During this stage, the individual makes a strong contribution to society and the world, through his own creativity or productivity—including the *pro*creativity of bringing another generation of children into the world.

Late Adult Stage: Fifty-five Years Old and Beyond
(Task: Integrity)

This stage represents the final stage of one's life, in which individuals accomplish the task of cementing integrity and wholeness. This means, ideally, that they can look back on their life with few regrets. A person who has successfully negotiated all of the preceding stages is able to feel good about himself, about God, and about others. This individual is a fulfilled individual awaiting the destiny of his own mortality.

A diagram of Erickson's stages of personality development gives us a pyramidal view of an entire human life.

Stages of Personality Development

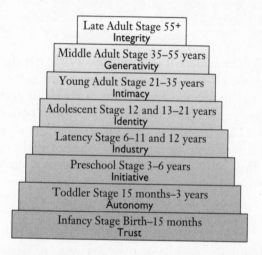

This is an idealized model. We don't all negotiate each of these stages with equal success and arrive at full emotional maturity. If the process breaks down at some stage, if we fail to complete our tasks of personality development, then the result is a person who is chronologically mature but emotionally immature or stunted. The diagram on the next page shows the contrast between individuals with mature personality structure (on the left) versus those with immature personality structure (on the right).

Mature and Immature Personality Structures

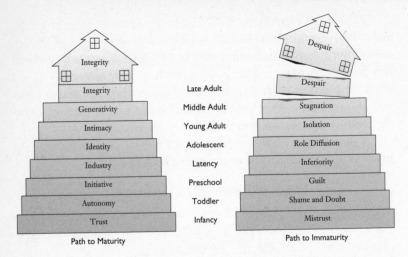

Path to Maturity		Path to Immaturity
Integrity	Late Adult	Despair
Generativity	Middle Adult	Stagnation
Intimacy	Young Adult	Isolation
Identity	Adolescent	Role Diffusion
Industry	Latency	Inferiority
Initiative	Preschool	Guilt
Autonomy	Toddler	Shame and Doubt
Trust	Infancy	Mistrust

What is personality? It is simply the way in which an individual has grown to think, feel, and respond to the world and to his or her feelings at any one given point in time. For example, children who are on the path toward an immature personality may become impulsive (meaning they cannot delay gratification when they feel frustrated inside), making decisions without thinking. Therefore they respond to parents and rules in a way that causes them to be overly controlled or disciplined by their parents, which creates even more frustration in their attitude about themselves, their adult caretakers, and their world.

On the other hand, children who are on the path toward a mature personality will have a strong sense of trust that their needs will be met in due time, and will have achieved a sense of internal control when dealing with frustrated feelings. They will have a more positive experience with parents, with discipline, with boundaries, and with other authorities, thereby creating a positive attitude about themselves and about life.

As your child goes through each of these stages, remember that he will have various drives and specific needs that must be satisfied. For example, in the first fifteen months of life, your child needs to feel loved and secure. These needs are satisfied by you, the parent, through the relationship between you and your child. As these basic needs are satisfied and the developmental tasks are accomplished one by one, another level or floor of the personality structure is added for the next stage of your child's personality development.

It is important to realize that the duration of each of these stages is an approximation. Different children pass through these stages at different rates, and there are also periods of regression (slipping back into a prior stage), periods of cessation (being stuck in a stage for a while), and periods of strong, aggressive growth accompanied by periods of intense stress and frustration. Development does not occur at the same rate of speed in all the five areas of growth—physical, mental, relational, emotional, and spiritual. For example, a twenty-five-year-old adult may be a genius mentally, be perfect physically, and yet habitually react at the preschool level emotionally, exhibiting behavior such as throwing temper tantrums when he doesn't get his way in his marriage. Such a person is demonstrating emotionally immature behavior.

What would cause an individual to take the path leading to immaturity? This individual most likely had some difficulty completing the developmental tasks between the infancy and toddler stages, where the original crack in the character structure would have originated. Perhaps this individual never learned healthy ways to handle early feelings of frustration from mom and dad, or had parents who were emotionally immature and unable to effectively love and discipline him. Because of this crack in the early foundation of this person's personality, when frustration in the marriage relationship develops, problems are almost inevitable. Where personality is concerned, early cracks in a person's foundation can cause one's personality to topple later in life.

Our task, as parents, is to give our children a sound and strong foundation upon which to build a healthy, reliable personality. If we do this at the same time that we are imparting the stories and principles of our faith, then the likelihood is that our children will develop a healthy, trusting relationship with God.

"Let's Talk to Jesus"

HANNA REACHED DOWN, SCOOPED Jenea up off the floor, and
dashed to the kitchen sink without a break in stride. Instantly she
had cold water running and was bathing her daughter in the
stream from the tap. Jenea would scream hard and loud for several seconds, then suck in a huge, long, silent breath and scream
again. "Sweetie, tell Mommy where it hurts!" ordered Hanna
when her daughter paused for a breath.

"Care me, Momma!" Jenea wailed.

"I'm taking care of you, sweetheart," Hanna responded, driz-
zling cold water over her hair and arms. "Just tell me where it
hurts, so I can make it feel better!"

"Cake care me, Momma!"

"I'm taking care of you, sweetie! Just tell me—"

"No! Cake care me! Cake care me!"

"What? . . . Oh! The cake scared you, honey?"

"Uh-huh."

"Did the cake hurt you?"

"Not hurt. Care me."

"You're not hurt? It just scared you?"

"Uh-huh. No more water, Momma. No more water."

Hanna turned off the water and slumped down to the kitchen
floor, holding Jenea in her arms. Suddenly she felt very weak—
and very relieved. She looked over to the breakfast nook, where
the two cake halves lay broken and steaming next to the table. She
hugged her daughter tightly to herself.

"Mommy mad?" asked Jenea.

"No," said Hanna, "Mommy's not mad. Mommy's happy that
Jenea is all right. Let's talk to Jesus and thank him for protecting
you. Jesus took good care of you and kept you from getting hurt."

"Jesus! Jesus!"

"Dear Jesus," Hanna prayed, "thank you for keeping Jenea from
getting hurt. Thank you that you love us. Thank you that you are
like a mommy and daddy to us, and you watch over us all the time."

Jenea put her hands together. "Thank you, Jesus," she said
with her head bowed but her eyes glancing back at the mess in

the breakfast nook. "Cake care me, Jesus. Thank you, Jenea not hurt myself, Jesus. Thank you, Jesus."

"Amen," said Hanna.

"Aaaaaaaaaa-men! Yaaaaayyyyyy!" Jenea wriggled in her mother's arms, pointing to the scattered fragments of cake on the floor. "Cake now! Cake now!"

"No," said Hanna with a sigh. "Cake *tomorrow*. And a *bakery* cake this time."

The Stages of Cognitive (Mental) Development

IN THE EARLY 1900s, most educators viewed intelligence as the amount of knowledge a person had stored and how fast that person could learn. They thought intelligence was fixed at birth; therefore, it didn't grow. By the mid-1900s it was generally assumed that intelligence grew by degrees, until child development researcher Jean Piaget suggested that intelligence actually grows in stages, and that it is a task not of *adding* to the mind but rather of *transforming* the mind, like the change from a caterpillar to a butterfly. He identified four basic stages of cognitive and intellectual development that one experiences throughout life. These stages have strong implications for the spiritual growth of children.

Sensory Motor Stage (Ages Birth to Two)

From birth to about the age of two, a child learns through a feeling-action response to the external environment, human and physical. The infant makes sense of the world primarily through physical observation—that is, by seeing, hearing, and touching.

Preoperational Stage (Ages Two to Seven)

When the child can speak, a second stage has been reached, characterizing the early childhood years from two to seven. Now there is the possibility of talking to others. Words can be internalized to become thoughts. The child can reflect on behavior. Actions can also become internalized. This means the child can develop relationships with, and feelings about, other people. Whereas the infant's task was to relate to and understand the physical environment, the young child now faces a new task: socialization (social interaction with others). At this stage there is a new capacity to make sense of the world, through language and imagination. Preschoolers learn through intuition rather than through systematic logic, and they have a creative imagination.

Concrete Operations Stage (Approximately Ages Seven to Eleven)

This stage brings about a substantial cognitive development. Children are clearly able to differentiate the self from others and to engage in cooperative endeavors. They understand relationships between objects. Intuition has become transformed into operational thinking in terms of visualizing concrete situations. For example, a child is shown two sticks of identical length lying horizontally parallel on a table. When one is moved slightly to the right of the other but is still parallel, the preschool child will say that one is longer than the other. The seven- to eight-year-old will know that they are still the same size and that only the position has been changed. This illustrates the principle of reversibility. Older children understand that the place of the sticks can be changed without changing their size. The elementary-school-age child has a new capacity at this stage to use mental logic but is limited to situations that are real and observable. Children at this stage learn facts easily, are very literal, and see social issues in terms of black and white, right and wrong.

Formal Operations Stage (Often Ages Eleven and Up)

From about age eleven to age twelve, the child enters the stage of abstract thinking—the ability to conceptualize what adults do when they speak of thinking. Only at adolescence and into adulthood can a person construct theories and systems and become able to philosophize or theologize. This is hypothetical and deductive thinking. Reflection becomes possible and ideas become exciting. The learner can see the possible as well as the immediate, can see what might be as well as what is. In adolescence and adulthood, an important way of making sense of the world is through abstract thinking. Now there is the ability to solve hypothetical problems with logical thinking. Piaget found that growth is promoted through interaction with other children and with parents. Progress in development is motivated or enhanced as a child encounters and resolves perplexing situations. The theories of Piaget have provided invaluable insights for teaching children about God and the Bible. He would suggest that we encourage young people to struggle with problems, rather than give them easy answers. He would also suggest that we give children plenty of opportunity to explore for themselves and to interact with other children. The implications of this particular theory for the development of your child's faith and spiritual growth will be discussed in future chapters.

The Stages of Moral Development

THE FOURTH AND FINAL dimension of spiritual growth is moral development, a process described by Lawrence Kohlberg, who observed that people move from one stage of moral development to another. By successfully negotiating these stages, an individual moves toward moral maturity. Kohlberg noted that these stages of moral development are not rigidly defined. A person in one stage will sometimes act in accordance with a lower stage of moral thinking, and at other times act as if in the higher stage. There is no timetable as to how long one will remain in a stage, but no one ever skips a stage.

Kohlberg revolutionized the understanding of moral reasoning, theorizing that the way children reason about moral issues develops in stages based on cognitive (thinking) ability. Kohlberg developed his theory by interviewing young people and posing moral dilemmas to them. He was interested not so much in their answers to these dilemmas as in the reasons for their answers. He found that young people move through three stages in their moral reasoning.

Preconventional Stage

The first stage is selfishly oriented. The motivation for choosing right or wrong is based on the physical consequences of the action. When children are motivated by a fear of punishment or by a desire for reward, they evidence this first stage. Children at this stage may picture God as a police officer or as Santa Claus. Younger children, grades one to six, tend to fall into the preconventional stage. They are trying to keep the rules. They understand specific meanings for good and bad, right and wrong, with reference to how authority figures define the terms.

There are two subtly defined levels to this stage. In the first level, around ages six and seven, the child tends to obey rules in order to avoid punishment. The concern of the child is not for morality or respect for authority; the object is simply to avoid painful consequences. But in the second level, around ages eight and nine, the child begins to obey in order to satisfy needs, such as the need to be approved, accepted, and rewarded.

Conventional Stage

The second stage of moral reasoning is oriented more toward society than toward self. Right or wrong depends on social convention. Motivation for doing the right thing is to please the peer group or the rules of society. Motivation for Christian living may be based on the need for a sense of belonging to a caring group. Individuals in this stage are developing the feeling of loyalty to the family, school, peer group, or community, as well as a sense of identity within the group.

Postconventional Stage

The third, or postconventional, stage may also be referred to as the autonomous stage or the principle stage. The motivation for moral reasoning here is based on universal principles of justice, rather than interest in the rules of society. This is the highest stage of moral development and is exemplified, said Kohlberg, by the high moral ethic of the Golden Rule. This stage is only possible when people have attained sufficient cognitive development to make reasonable decisions. It could not be expected of a preadolescent individual.

This stage embodies universal principles of justice and respect for individuals, and it is the goal toward which we, as Christian parents, seek to raise our children. There are two practical things we can remember to help us promote moral development in our children.

Children move to higher stages of moral development when they sense that they are part of a just, moral, and ethical community. Therefore it is important that we operate on the highest principles of morality, not only toward our children but toward others, so that our children can see and imitate the high moral standards we have set for ourselves. Obviously, we're human and we make mistakes, but we should always show our children that our goal is to live lives of integrity.

Years ago a father received a letter from his college-age son. "Hey, Dad," the letter began, "this letter is free. The post office didn't cancel the stamp on your last letter, so I reused it." Soon afterward the son received an answer from his dad. Unfolding the letter, he found a stamp at the top, with a big, bold X scrawled across it. Beneath that were the words, "Dear Son, your debt to the United States Government has been paid." Here was a father who understood the meaning of high moral principles and who worked creatively at communicating those principles to his son so that his son could be brought to the third and highest stage of moral development.

Children move to higher stages of moral development when they sense they are free to discuss and work through their everyday moral dilemmas. As parents, we should create the kind of open, accepting, affirming home environment in which a child can feel free to ask questions and discuss issues such as truthfulness, peer pressure, drugs, sex, questionable moral content of entertainment and educational media, and so forth. Parents should be unshockable so children always feel comfortable talking about problem issues and so they feel that parents are friends who can be trusted to help them sort through moral choices and moral principles.

"I Hope She Doesn't Forget"

JENEA SLEPT PEACEFULLY WHILE Hanna and Scott stood on either side of her bed.

"I was so frightened," said Hanna. "I thought she was going to be burned, scarred for life. I only had my back turned for a second, and there she was, pulling those hot cake pans down on herself. It was a miracle she wasn't hurt."

"It's too bad about your cake—all that work," said Scott.

"Oh, I don't care about that," said Hanna. "As long as our little one is OK, that's all I care about. God really watched out for her. Poor little thing was so scared."

"I hope Jenea can forget all about it and just have a great birthday tomorrow."

"You know what, Scott?" said Hanna. "I hope she doesn't forget it."

"Huh? Oh, you mean so she won't pull cake pans down off the table again?"

"Well, that too. But I think Jenea learned something even more important today. She learned that Jesus is right here in our family, right alongside us, with us all the time. The moment the crisis was past, I just sat down on the floor with Jenea and we talked to Jesus, the two of us. It was so real, so natural, thanking Jesus for being here and for helping us. I want to be more conscious of opportunities like that. I want to take time every now and then to simply pause with Jenea and thank Jesus for the sunshine or for music or just for happy moments. I want her to feel that God is always right here with her and that she can turn to him and talk to him at any time, for any reason or for no reason at all. I think Jenea learned something of that today. And I think I did, too."

SEVEN

Total Personality and Emotional Growth

FLASH BACK IN TIME, twenty-one years ago. Joanna Brown is a young mother suffering from clinical depression. Her baby boy, only two months old, has been crying in the crib in his room for over an hour while she lies on the couch with her hands over her eyes. She is scarcely able to think, much less move to help her baby. The only thoughts she has are of what a dull, darkened hole her life has become.

Her mother died just weeks before baby Michael was born. Her husband's business is failing, and there's scarcely enough money to keep food on the table. The phone has been turned off, and the gas company has left a twenty-four-hour cutoff notice on the door. Her baby cries all the time, and she is unable to adequately care for him. Joanna and her husband, J. W., have no close friends since leaving their previous church after an ugly doctrinal split.

This, she thinks, *is what my life has become—lonely, deprived, full of pressure, fear, and stress—and this is what it will be from now on. Things will never get better.* This kind of hopeless thinking reinforces her pain and her depression.

Just then, five-year-old Hanna comes up to the couch where Joanna lies, tugging at Joanna's sleeve. "Momma, Mikey's crying! Make him be quiet!"

"I can't," Joanna mumbles. "I can't. Leave me alone."

A room away, baby Michael wails louder.

"Momma!" Hanna repeats, tugging more insistently. "Mikey's crying!"

Suddenly Joanna reaches out and grips Hanna's pudgy wrist, squeezing. "I *know* Mikey's crying! I *hear* him crying! I can't do anything about it, so GO AWAY!"

Hanna runs away, crying even louder than her brother. Joanna sinks into a deeper gloom.

Life Development Curves: Infancy Through Preschool

THERE ARE MANY FACTORS that can interfere with a child's emotional development throughout life. The final outcome of each life curve stage is crucial in your child's development, because these curves represent milestones in his maturation. They also represent forks in the road for your child's journey toward socialization (the ability to love and interact with self, life, and others in a healthy way), therefore the path that he chooses or is led down by you will have profound implications for his future.

At this point it is important to remember the following distinctions: personality growth describes how a child handles life at surface level; emotional growth describes how a child experiences life at a deeper level. Personality breakdown can lead to emotional breakdown and vice versa. The following diagram illustrates the different curves or paths a personality may take in the earliest stages of personality development, from birth to six years of age.

In this diagram, you can see how important it is to give children a healthy emotional experience, from the earliest stages of their development. Each successfully completed development stage moves them to a higher level of emotional health so they can continue their movement toward socialization. If a child successfully moves through these development stages from infancy to preschool, he should end up being able to love life, love self, and love others in a healthy way.

Each development stage that is not successfully completed sends the child on a downward path toward shame, guilt, low self-esteem, and anger. A child who has these poisonous emotions coursing through his personality has many more emotional obstacles to overcome in order to experience a healthy relationship with self and with others. Normal children will experience either

Mature and Immature Life Development Curves
(Infancy through Preschool 0–6 years old)

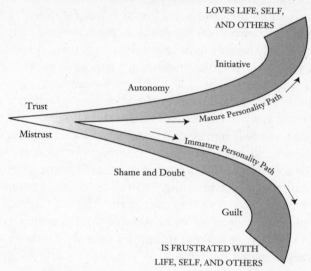

LOVES LIFE, SELF, AND OTHERS

Initiative

Autonomy

Trust

Mature Personality Path

Mistrust

Immature Personality Path

Shame and Doubt

Guilt

IS FRUSTRATED WITH LIFE, SELF, AND OTHERS

extreme of the life development curves while growing; however, at some point, usually by age six, a definite outlook on self and life will develop into a pattern.

Let's take a closer look at these life development curves, stage by stage.

Infancy Stage: Trust vs. Mistrust

The importance of the life experience that your child has during the first fifteen months of life cannot be overstated. A child's capacity to view life as a positive experience is greatly affected by how his primary caregivers treat him during the first fifteen months of life. The infant child receives his basic sense of pleasure and security through food, warmth, and cuddling. So the degree to which you, the parent, meet these needs—consistently, gently, and lovingly—largely determines whether or not your infant experiences you as a positive or negative object in his world. The more consistently you meet the child's needs, the more fully the child begins to trust and internalize you.

Once your child has internalized you as a positive object, you will tend to remain a positive object in his mind. This positive experience will affect not only your later relationship with your child but, more importantly, his future relationship with God. If your child experiences you as a positive object in these early years, he will probably be able to have good feelings toward you even if later in your parent-child relationship you have to say, "I can't meet all your needs right now; you have to wait."

If, however, you fail to meet the pleasure and security needs of your child early in life, he will likely internalize you as a negative object. You will represent to your child someone who is not safe to be around, not nurturing, not loving, not someone who is willing or able to meet his dependency needs. This negative experience will also affect his ability to relate to other people in a secure, trusting way. As a therapist at the Minirth Clinic, I constantly encounter adults whose relationships are distorted or made painful in large part because infant dependency needs were not adequately satisfied by parents. When the capacity for trust is impaired, relationships become much more difficult.

The process of healthy, positive internalization is best achieved through consistent, repeated close physical and emotional contact between the infant and his parents, particularly with the mother. A child whose needs are ignored or frustrated in infancy will often grow to adulthood wondering, *Why can't I experience trusting, satisfying relationships?*

Toddler Stage: Autonomy vs. Shame and Doubt

The inner world of a toddler is an emotional hurricane. The parents may experience the frustrations of "the terrible twos," but this is also a difficult time for the child—and an extremely sensitive growth period in the child's life. The toddler interacts with his world and his parents in an intense, resistant, and reactive way. At around fifteen months of age, he undergoes a difficult stage that psychologists call *separation individuation*. This natural developmental milestone is characterized by the child's attempt to gain a sense of personal autonomy. It is completely normal during this stage for the toddler to be obstinate and negative. The child will also be an extremely messy individual to be around, since he is just beginning toilet training and learning to feed himself. He feels strong emotions and expresses both love and hate, as well as an aggressive drive to take on the developmental tasks of this stage.

Parents need to remember (but most forget) that toddlers are limited in their ability to understand and communicate what they are feeling and experiencing. Toddlers are caught in the classic "push me–pull you" dilemma: they want freedom and autonomy, yet they also want love and security. This dilemma is guaranteed to produce at least a year or two of potentially strong conflict between you and your toddler.

The combination of the child's strong emotions, inner conflicts, and limited communication skills makes it difficult for a parent to know how to respond: *Should I say yes or no? Should I be patient or firm?* Too much control, and the child becomes frustrated; too much freedom, and the child will feel insecure and unloved. Parents should strive for that wise, loving balance between freedom and limits, since either excessive control or excessive permissiveness can produce confusion in the child as he seeks to separate himself from his parents in a healthy way and discover his own individuality.

A child fortunate enough to be successful at the task of achieving autonomy in the toddler years will experience a sense of being a distinct person with his own thoughts, his own feelings, and his own opinions. He will have a healthy concept of his own self-worth and self-esteem. The child who is secure in his own thoughts and identity can allow for the thoughts and feelings of others—an important step toward being socialized. A child who grows up uncertain about his individual identity often displays either excessive inhibition or aggressiveness, experiences poor self-esteem and feelings of being unlovable or worthless, and may resist socialization.

It is crucial that toddlers successfully complete two tasks of this stage of development: (1) the construction of a healthy sense of self-esteem, and (2) the development of a healthy respect for authority. Both of these tasks are largely influenced by how the child's parents respond to him. The child learns how to view himself and how to view authority from interacting with his parents. They teach him how to respect himself and how to respect their own authority. The manner in which the toddler is treated by the parents communicates to him that he is either lovable and worthwhile—or unlovable and unworthy. The parents are also the first people who attempt to place controls or boundaries on the child, and their challenge is to shape his will without breaking his self-esteem.

The temptation in this stage is to overuse the word *no*. If you block a child's desires, curiosity, and interests at every turn, he will eventually decide that it is not worth it to try to establish his own identity—and that he doesn't deserve to have his wishes fulfilled. Some parents impose such tight behavior constraints on a child, telling him no at every turn and with every move, that the child soon feels he's in a box. There's nothing he can do that's legal. This is a sure way to destroy a child emotionally and to cause him to resent his parents when he grows up. Instead of continually saying no to their toddler, parents should seek creative ways of saying yes, of setting boundaries that are healthy yet slightly elastic. The child should be allowed to explore his own capabilities and curiosities, so long as he does not harm himself or others.

Preschool Stage: Initiative vs. Guilt

During this aggressive growth period, at approximately three to six years of age, the child rockets forward developmentally, as his God-given drive and motivation for emotional and psychological growth is triggered. If the child has successfully negotiated the previous two stages of development, he is ready to learn new skills for positively relating to family members and his world. At this stage, children start exploring their surroundings. They become extremely curious, wanting to see and do *everything*. Their communication skills grow, and they ask questions about *everything*.

At this time of unbridled exploration, children live rich fantasy lives and may exhibit profound exaggeration at times. Some theorists suggest that the greater the intellectual potential of the child, the more active the child's fantasy life. An active fantasy life is natural—but there are risks. To be mature, one must live in the real world and be able to separate fantasy from both internal and external reality.

A child at this level of maturation is hungry for parental approval—and the failure to receive adequate parental approval now may create emotional deficits or voids that last into adulthood, causing the individual to go through his adult life feeling unworthy and unsatisfied—always hungering for the approval of others.

The approval you give your child should be used as a steering mechanism for this rocket that is firing within his being. You can steer it in a positive direction—or you can steer it along a negative curve. What happens if parental approval is withheld? Perfectionistic or overcontrolling parents sometimes expect too much of a child, frustrating the child, causing the child to develop self-defeating feelings: *Even the best I can do is not acceptable; why try?* At that point, the child's drive to learn, grow, explore, create, aspire, and achieve is shut down.

During this time of self-exploration, your child is also going through a sexual crisis as he discovers differences between males and females. The child may feel a deep anxiety as he attempts to deal with the ambiguity he experiences between understanding his own body and understanding the differences he sees in the opposite sex. It is not uncommon to hear sexual questions from your child or to catch your child in sex play and various forms of peeking. This is normal behavior, and if you punish or shame your child for this normal curiosity, the child will be made to feel bad or abnormal and may learn to associate normal feelings with abnormality or sin. The child's normal sexual development and identity could be hindered or harmed at this stage.

During the preschool years your child gains a realization of what it means to be a member of a family. For the first three years, his relationship with mom is the most important. It is frequently a rather exclusive relationship, in part because of the child's needs and in part because the child normally spends more time with mom during those early years. Dad, however, has an important role to play in the child's life and development.

As the child observes the marriage relationship between mom and dad, it is very normal for him, as the smallest part of this threesome, to feel insecure or left out. The child will often deal with this developmental crisis by trying to insert himself into a more prominent position in the triangle. As a result, he may become jealous of dad for mom's attention. (A little girl, on the other hand, sometimes becomes jealous of mom and may want dad all to herself.) The child does not consciously understand his own feelings and should not be reprimanded for this normal behavior. He is just trying to find and establish a place in the family, and parents should respond by validating the child's worth and affirming their love for the child.

The good news about the preschool stage is that children begin to develop self-discipline—the ability to say no to themselves. The child develops this self-discipline through the process of internalizing *your* discipline. When you discipline consistently, when your no means no and your yes means yes, when the child is able to make sense of the boundaries you impose, he is able to develop a conscience. If the child is able to internalize you, the parent, as a positive object in his life, he is more likely to internalize your discipline and instruction as a good thing in his life. Then when confronted with a choice between right and wrong, the child is more likely to choose what is right, even though the wrong is enticing. He will have learned to trust that even though the right choice may not be as gratifying in the immediate moment, it will produce greater benefit in his life. He will accept your boundaries, because he accepts you.

It is important to understand that internally your child is egocentric and not fully capable of understanding the abstract principle of delayed gratification. He thinks rewards should come immediately and not later. Therefore he will try to manipulate you into giving immediate gratification whenever he hears the word *no*. These attempts at changing your mind when he wants something are part of the testing process between you and your child. This is normal. Your child needs to test the rule before he internalizes it. It may seem to take forever for your child to internalize rules and demonstrate self-discipline. But if you are consistent, loving yet firm, he will eventually be able to internalize your rules.

Consistency is crucial in this stage. Consistency got your child through the first two stages, and it will get him through this stage. Parents who are inconsistent in setting boundaries and showing love to their child become a roadblock to the child's ability to internalize their rules. This can have a profound effect on the child's later ability to internalize the loving discipline of God as the child begins to formulate a relationship with God.

The greatest obstacle to your child's successful navigation through this developmental journey is something called guilt. Feelings of guilt are common and normal for this stage but must be handled sensitively and with care. The conflict between the competing drives for dependence and independence—a conflict that began in the previous stage—continues in this stage. The child is frustrated that certain needs are delayed or unmet and feels resentment toward you. This is natural. At the same time, he loves you and needs you and feels that his anger and resentment are unacceptable. He takes this as proof that he is a bad person. He feels guilty. He feels he cannot share these feelings because he may be rejected, abandoned, or punished. So he learns to repress his anger so he can continue to function normally in the relationship.

As all this is going on, your child is still competing for your love (a son competes for mom's love, and a daughter for dad's love), and this stimulates even more guilt within your child. If we, as parents, understand the guilt and anger our children feel, we can help them to successfully resolve these feelings.

Picture this scenario: Dad and Mom are sitting at the table, paying monthly bills. Dad writes checks while Mom puts the checks into envelopes and addresses them. Five-year-old Jenny comes up, climbs into Dad's lap, and says, "Let me help!" Dad's arm is jostled, he ruins a check, and in annoyance he says, "Jenny, get away. Go in the other room and play!" This generates frustration and anger within this little girl—yet she also feels guilty over her anger, even though she doesn't understand her feelings. She is angry with the ones who are supposed to love her and whom she is supposed to love—those who take care of her. These are unacceptable feelings, so she also feels guilt. She feels additional guilt over an unconscious rivalry with Mom. Though she can't under-stand her feelings, much less communicate them, these feelings are real, and she may express them by screaming, crying, pouting, or going into Mom and Dad's bedroom and breaking something. Here's a possible solution: Dad could pause from his work, give his child an affirming hug, look his child in the eye (eye commu-nication is very important in conveying affirmation and a sense of worth to a child), and say, "Thank you for wanting to help Mommy and Daddy pay the bills. Let's have you sit in this chair by Mommy and Daddy. Here's a crayon, and I want you to mark these envelopes with these crayons and put these slips of paper in them, and that will make Mommy and Daddy very pleased, because you are helping us do our work." This is a way of turning down the child's offer of "help" by actually saying yes to the child. Dad gives the child a sense of self-control and affirmation, and builds up the child's sense of self-worth—even while sticking to his own adult agenda of getting the bills paid. He avoids placing the child in the "push me–pull you" trap of frustration and guilt.

This is not to say that guilt is always a negative force. A cer-tain sense of "positive guilt," or conscience, should be encouraged in a child as a healthy response to sin, so that the child can develop self-control. But all too often children feel a false and unnecessary guilt over their normal developmental responses and natural emo-tions—and as parents, we want to do all we can to free our chil-dren from the clutches of self-defeating misplaced guilt.

Another source of guilt feelings in children is their inability to control their own frustrations, leading to explosions of anger. It is not uncommon for preschool-age children to become so angry and frustrated by their parents that they would even momentar-ily wish their parents were gone or dead. This may sound shock-ing, but it shouldn't be—young children, after all, scarcely have any conception of what "dead" means. Along with these angry, frustrated feelings comes the fear that their angry wishes might actually become reality—and the guilt over having such feelings. Children at this stage often go through a process of *projective inter-nalization*—the magical belief that they have the power to deter-mine events by their strong feelings. This is why so many children feel guilty over a death, a separation, or a divorce; they think that it was their feelings or behavior that somehow caused the tragedy, and they feel enormous, crushing guilt as a result. It is especially important that when tragic events befall the family, parents pay attention to what their preschool children are feeling and make sure that their children know that they are not in any way responsible for the sad or tragic events.

The preschool stage is the make-or-break stage for the development of self-control, emotional coping skills, and a healthy self-esteem. Your child learns how to respond to his own feelings by seeing how you respond to his feelings. If your child sees that you respond by accepting him even when his feelings are angry and frustrated, if he sees that you are patient with him even when you disagree with his feelings, then he will learn to accept himself and be patient with himself. He will have a sense of healthy self-worth even when things are not going well in his world or in his emotions. But if you respond by rejecting him when he is angry or frustrated, he will grow up feeling shamed, unacceptable, and unworthy because of his emotions. Ultimately he will tend to have even less control over his emotions and his behavior, because his shame, guilt, and other negative emotions will magnify whatever he is feeling and cause him to react explosively rather than in a healthy, controlled way.

Preschool children tend to deal with feelings of frustration, anger, and guilt in three ways: (1) by being destructive to others (losing control, lashing out); (2) by provoking reactions from others (expressing feelings in such a way as to provoke parental anger or discipline); or (3) by being self-punishing (bottling up feelings, blaming themselves, thinking bad thoughts about themselves). Many children, in order to avoid receiving punishment or overt expressions of anger from parents, adopt *passive-aggressive* methods of provoking or manipulating their parents. Passive aggression is an attempt to annoy, anger, or control another person without risking open conflict or confrontation. Passive-aggressive behavior may include sulking (while denying anything is wrong), procrastination, laziness, ignoring, complaining, and engaging in irritating, aggravating behavior while being careful not to cross the line that would invite open conflict. All of these are unhealthy ways of dealing with negative feelings.

Parents can help their children to express their anger and frustration in healthy ways, by tuning in to what their children are feeling, by attempting to see the world through their eyes and feel the world through their feelings, and by teaching them to accept themselves and to talk through their feelings. For example, "I know you're feeling very angry and upset that we can't go to the park today. Even though I can't allow you to yell like that, I want you to know that I don't blame you one bit for feeling disappointed and angry. In fact, I remember when I was your age, something like that happened to me. . . ." Convey to the child that you understand and identify with his feelings but that you also expect him to manage and control his behavioral responses to those feelings.

Life Development Curves: Latency Through Adolescence

THE NEXT CRUCIAL LIFE development curve your child will encounter occurs from latency into adolescence. The mature and immature life development curves for latency through adolescence are depicted below.

The essence of this diagram can be summed up in two words: confidence and wholeness. As you can see, the child who grows upward along the mature personality path, having already attained the ability to love and trust, has now achieved enough self-confidence to find himself, his purpose and meaning in life. Through getting his needs met, he can experience wholeness.

At the opposite extreme, we find the dead end road of the immature life development curve. The conclusion of a child's journey down this path is basically insecurity and emptiness. Since the child who has taken this path has no self-confidence, he finds himself handicapped or almost paralyzed at the door to wholeness. He is not sure who he is, because of a lack of accomplishments; he can't find his role, in that he has no meaningful relationships; and he can't find meaning in life because he can't get any of his needs met. Let's try to gain a better understanding of the two development stages of this life curve.

Mature and Immature Life Development Curves
(Latency through Adolescence 6–21 years old)

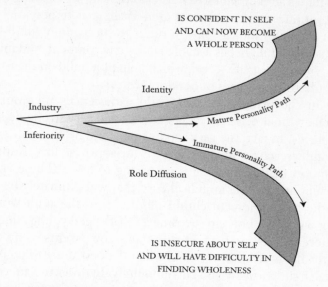

IS CONFIDENT IN SELF
AND CAN NOW BECOME
A WHOLE PERSON

Identity

Industry

Inferiority

Mature Personality Path

Immature Personality Path

Role Diffusion

IS INSECURE ABOUT SELF
AND WILL HAVE DIFFICULTY IN
FINDING WHOLENESS

Latency Stage: Industry vs. Inferiority

The latency stage involves the elementary school years, approximately ages six to twelve, and is characterized by the developmental growth task of industry. The industrious drive of the latent stage is an extension of a child's continuing drive for learning, from the previous stage, combined with the strong progressive drive toward independence, begun at around fifteen months. A child who has successfully completed the developmental tasks of the previous three stages should now be able to deal with excessive guilt, fear, and anger, and should be free to progress to future stages, without any serious emotional hindrances to overcome. During this stage, the child prepares to leave home for school—and though separation from parents and family is stressful, he has built a firm foundation for the transition into preadolescence.

The big step of adult independence actually begins in this stage, with a lot of smaller steps. The child gradually transitions from home to the world around him, spending half of his days in school with other people. The child undergoes changes as influences of schoolteachers and peers are superimposed on feelings and attitudes already acquired in the home. During this stage, the child continues to have a strong God-given growth potential for being creative or industrious. In order to successfully fulfill this potential, the child needs a stable family environment, and interaction with the outside world, which help him build on the foundation of previous stages of development.

As in the prior stage, the child experiences the conflict between an inner drive for independence and very strong dependency needs. In fact, the very support the child needs in order to successfully reach for independence is the approval, love, respect, and support of the home he is preparing to leave. These emotional supports are the umbilical cord that will ultimately be cut when the postadolescent child is "born" into the adult world, moving out of the house to become a full-fledged young adult.

There is a temptation, at this stage, for parents to do too much for the preadolescent child when the best thing to do is to stand back supportively and encouragingly. In order to gain confidence, young people need to build a repertoire of success experiences, proving to themselves that they can handle life as they move up the life development curve. But to build well-rounded self-esteem and self-confidence, they need more than a string of successes. They need the *freedom to fail*—and to know that they are still loved, still accepted, still okay.

During this passage of early life, children switch from competing with the same-sex parent (as in the prior stage) to patterning themselves after the same-sex parent. If the previous stages have been successfully negotiated, the child reaches this stage confident of being loved and accepted by the same-sex parent, and in turn seeks to emulate the admired traits of this parent. If, however, the child doubts the same-sex parent's love and approval, he is likely to reject this parent as a role model—and may even try to do the extreme opposite of all that this parent says and does.

During this sensitive time of maturation children also deal with the issue of sexual identity, so it is extremely important that parents model good sex-role behaviors and attitudes, and demonstrate satisfaction with their own sexual identities and roles. Early in this stage, there is some normal vacillation regarding preferred sex role. However, toward the end of this stage, children usually accept their sexual identity with pride.

During ages six to twelve, family identity is further defined for the child. Mom and dad model marriage and parenthood as either worthwhile and gratifying or hopeless and disappointing. Family experiences also serve to shape the child's view of God and spirituality: if spiritual values are taught in a home environment that is positive and happy, then the child will tend to have a positive view of God and faith; spiritual values that are imparted to children in a household characterized by abuse, neglect, abandonment, or extreme conflict will tend to create a negative perception of God and faith, and the child could find reasons to reject Christianity in adulthood.

The latency years are normally marked by an increase in the child's ability to demonstrate self-discipline and self-control—the continuation of a process begun in earlier stages. Your child should develop a sense of duty and accomplishment in schoolwork and should develop healthy relationships with school and neighborhood peers. You should also notice an increased ability to conform to the rules and values of society and of the family as his conscience develops.

The greatest obstacle to successfully completing the task of this stage is a sense of *inferiority*. As the diagram on page 121 shows, children in this stage are reaching toward industry; if they fail to complete this task, they arrive instead at a place of inferiority. Albert Adler, famous psychological theoretician, believed that all of us are born with inferiority feelings and that our goal in life is to deal with those feelings by becoming superior enough to feel equal with others. Failure to achieve that superiority leaves us in a lifelong state of feeling inferior.[1]

Excessive inferiority feelings are usually formed when a child is confronted with numerous self-defeating experiences or when the experiences in which he loses outweigh the experiences in which he wins. Often, in this stage of development, children who are extremely gifted or "superior" in some areas find themselves feeling extremely inferior. Why? Because they fail to please their parents, or they fail to achieve successful relationships with peers. It is so tragic to see children with enormous God-given potential robbed of their joy and satisfaction in life because of misplaced feelings of inferiority. Such children, feeling unacceptable to themselves, to parents, and to God, often experience confusion in their sexual identity, insecurity in their role at home, and rejection by peers. They often grow up self-centered and withdrawn, using self-defeating, unhealthy coping skills to make life bearable in an unbearable world. In a small but significant percentage of these children, self-internalized controls break down, and the child becomes extremely nonconformist or even antisocial (criminal).

ANOTHER FLASHBACK. THE TIME: nine years ago. The place: the bench behind the chain-link backstop of the softball diamond at Madison Elementary School. It's the bottom of the ninth, and young Michael's Little League team, the Cardinals, trails the Giants 12 to 14. There are two men on base (if you can call twelve-year-olds "men"), and one out. Ricky "the Stick" Sticklin leans over the plate as the ball is hurled—but Michael is not looking at the game. He is turned around, shading his eyes with one hand, scanning the bleachers. There are about half a dozen parents sitting there in the hot sun, cheering for their boys.

But Michael's dad isn't there. He promised to be there in time for the first pitch. Now it looks as if he won't even be there for the last out.

Ricky reaches with his bat, taking a pitch that comes in low and away—and surprisingly he connects, driving the ball in a high arc, straight into center field. At the *thock!* sound of ball on bat, Michael's head snaps around in time to see the Stick dashing for first base. The ball rises on the slight breeze, then falls . . .

Right into the glove of the Giants' center fielder, Josh Sawyer. Two away. The base runners return to their bases. It's Michael's turn at bat. He needs to get at least a solid base hit, or it's all over—and he's already struck out three times today.

Casting one last disappointed glance at the bleachers, Michael picks up an aluminum bat and heads for the batter's box ...

Adolescent Stage: Identity vs. Role Diffusion

The adolescent stage of emotional development includes the years from about twelve to twenty-one. The teenage years are crucial in the development of the child's sense of identity, the primary task of adolescence. During the adolescent years, the child wants to know, "Who am I? What is my purpose in life? What does it all mean?" During this stage, he must solidify himself as a *separate* person and a *worthwhile* person in society in order to attain successful transition into adulthood. The teenage search for identity and meaning is a universal, innate response to the drives placed within the child by God. A teenage child who does not achieve identity experiences role diffusion—a developmental quicksand wherein the child cannot grab hold of who he is, why he is here, and what life is about.

Your teenager's drive for independence is extremely powerful—and necessary. He must prove himself as a capable, autonomous individual as soon as possible—yet his drive for independence conflicts with the fact that he is still a child, still dependent on his parents. It is normal for teenagers to reach outside the family to seek their identity, looking to peers, teachers, sports figures, and media personalities as role models. Parents who are insecure and have trouble letting go may find this threatening and may respond by overcontrolling the child. It is important to understand what is going on within the child, to give him an increasing amount of freedom (as he shows he is able to handle it) while reassuring him that you, the parent, are always available for support, encouragement, help, and advice.

Adolescents crave the stability of unconditional acceptance as they pass through a kaleidoscope of unstable emotions, unstable behaviors, and unstable reactions. What do teenagers want in their parents? Someone to listen and understand those things they themselves don't understand. Someone to give them freedom to try their wings and learn by experience. Someone who will set reasonable boundaries and provide security and stability in their lives. While teenagers may rebel against rules, deep down they need and want rules. Teenagers respect parents who provide consistency and structure and who are united in their role.

The combination of strong adolescent drives plus inferiority feelings and unresolved conflicts from previous stages may result in an overtaxing of the child's internal controls, producing impulsive behavior or strong reaction to situations. Failure to develop socially acceptable expressions of independence and sexual impulses may result in a self-centered, lonely, isolated child. We can now clearly see how taking a mature path up the developmental life curve from the earliest stages facilitates the success of your child during the period of adolescence.

The Final Life Curves: Adult Life

WHEN YOUR CHILD HAS reached the development stage of adulthood, he has arrived at another crucial fork in the road. At this juncture only two basic paths may be taken. One path leads ultimately to a celebration, the other to regret, as the diagram below illustrates:

Mature and Immature Life Development Curves
(Adult Life 22–55+)

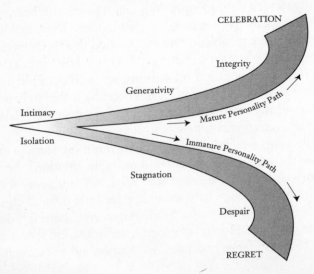

The adult who has consistently but not perfectly been able to follow the mature life development curves throughout childhood will most likely choose the final path that leads to celebration. Secure within himself, having completed the necessary prerequisite tasks, this adult has developed the capacity for intimacy with significant others, along with the ability to give to and receive from others on a mature basis; has experienced generativity—the ability to contribute to family and society through God-given talents, gifts, and through the gift of offspring. In turn, the rights of integrity and respect from significant others have been earned. Life is a celebration of close relationships, good memories, achievements, sentiments, family, and the gift of life as God had intended—one of joy, peace, and love through the good and the bad.

The child who has arrived at the road to adulthood developmentally handicapped will have a much more difficult time staying on the upward life curve toward celebration. This does not mean that only those who make a passing grade at every childhood development stage go on to have a good adult life—adults can make choices that can guide them toward a life of celebration. But this is difficult to do for many adults who have major cracks in their personality and emotional development.

Adults who are unable to or do not choose to make the climb along the upward life curve have no one close with whom to celebrate because they have never achieved intimacy. They have few accomplishments to celebrate because of their inability to give of themselves to others and society. They are often devoid of hope because of their despair over lifelong bankruptcy in the area of need fulfillment. What is left then at the end of this path? Mostly regret.

THE COUNT IS 2–2, and the ball comes speeding toward him, high and inside—so close that Michael flinches and pulls back, fearing that the ball is going to hit him. But he is even more afraid of losing the game on a called strike. He has to swing at it. Has to. So with his eyes screwed shut, he does.

Unbelieving, he hears the bat hammer the ball with a mighty *thwack!* He opens his eyes in time to see the ball torpedo the ground between third base and the pitcher's mound, then continue bounding toward left field. The runner from second has to jump over the streaking grounder as he heads for third. "Run, Mike, run!" says an adult voice at Michael's back. At first he thinks it is his dad, but as he takes off for first base, he realizes it is the voice of his coach.

The Giants' left fielder crouches to scoop up the ball as it bounces straight toward his open glove. Michael slows to hold up at first, thinking, *At least I got a base hit and didn't blow the game.* Then he sees the ball bounce off the fielder's glove and roll right between the fielder's legs. Michael speeds up, rounds first, and keeps on going.

The Giant fielder chases the ball, snags it, and throws to second—but the throw is about four feet over the second baseman's head. Michael keeps going, rounding second, heading for third. As he runs, the other two runners score, tying the game.

Somewhere along the right-side baseline, the pitcher comes up with the ball and sends it streaking toward third base. Michael and the ball arrive there at precisely the same moment—but the third baseman bobbles the ball, and Michael keeps going. The third baseman is still chasing the rolling ball, enduring the dismayed shouts of his teammates, as Michael crosses the plate, scoring the winning run.

The game is over. Michael's fellow Cardinals crowd around him, high-fiving him and mussing his hair. One last time, Michael scans the bleachers, looking for someone to share his triumph with. Looking for his father, who promised to be there.

Why does this moment of triumph feel so hollow and empty?

Parenting on God's Terms

THE GREATEST SPIRITUAL INFLUENCE a child will ever have is his parents. It may be a positive influence or a negative influence. In most cases, there is some mingling of the two. But no matter what kind of spiritual influence you choose to assert in the life of your child, no one will ever have a greater opportunity to mold and nourish and strengthen the faith of your child than you, the parent. And no one has more power to distort, damage, and weaken the faith of your child than you—not the New Age movement, secular humanism, the drug subculture, the education establishment, the cults, peers, nor the entertainment media.

The spiritual responsibility of parenthood is awesome beyond imagining. As Christian parents, we sometimes forget who our children truly belong to. Our children are not our possessions; they are placed in our care by God, the loving Father. They are his children and we are their guardians, and we must answer to him for our care and stewardship of these precious eternal lives.

Imagine how it would feel to hand your children over to a pair of young, inexperienced baby-sitters, knowing that they will be raising your children for the next twenty years. Imagine giving these baby-sitters instructions in how to care for your children, what to teach them, how to raise them. Imagine telling them, "Tell my children about me. Raise them as I would raise them myself. Show them what I am like. Make sure they know all about me and hear about me every day." How would you feel? What fears and worries would you have? Well, that is exactly how God felt when he entrusted his precious children to you.

God has blessed us with the opportunity to raise his children, to develop a lifelong relationship with his children, and to teach his children about himself. The parenting role is not something we deserve but something we have received as a gift of God's grace. When we perform our parenting role in such a way that we exemplify and model the character of God to our children, when we help to prepare these souls for a place in his kingdom, then we become partners in the eternal plan of God.

Unfortunately, all too few parents see the parenting role in this light. Many parents either ignore or consciously reject God's plan for raising children. They choose to parent their way rather than God's way, even though it was God the Father, the heavenly Parent, who designed and invented the parental role. If we choose to parent on our own terms instead of on God's terms, we are playing spiritual roulette with the eternal souls of our children.

Every day, I counsel patients who struggle in their faith because of childhood experiences in the home—and especially in Christian homes. Children learn trust—the experience of faith—through their relationship with their parents. *The emotional foundation for all their later spiritual growth has been laid (for better or for worse) during the first six years of life.* During the first six years of a child's life, his parents represent God in a powerful, symbolic way—and this relationship precedes, accompanies, and often overwhelms any formal religious training from church, Sunday school, vacation Bible school, or Christian school.

Children are not capable of setting their own spiritual course. They go in the direction that they are led. If we lead them astray by the example we set for them and the experience we create for them, then astray they will go. If we neglect our own relationship with God, we cannot point our children to a relationship with him. We cannot lead them where we ourselves have not gone. We cannot give them what we do not have.

In the story we have been following throughout this book, we have seen that J. W. Brown, father of Michael and Hanna, is a devout, Bible-believing man who is intensely involved in his church and who is a model citizen in his community. He believes that the way to pass on faith to his children is by *imparting information* to them—Bible verses and Bible stories and Bible principles. He truly feels that by giving his children biblical information, he is passing on his spiritual heritage to his children. It was not until his son, Michael, turned away from Christianity that J. W. learned that his way of transmitting the Christian faith was woefully inadequate.

As God's representatives to our children, it is imperative that we present an accurate portrayal of God to our children—not only through Scripture memory and sound doctrine but also through warm, loving, nurturing family experiences that reflect the warm, loving, nurturing character of God. As God's "baby-sitters," we are expected to parent our children on his terms. And what are God's terms for Christian parents? Here is a list.

- Give your children a continual experience of true unconditional love, forgiveness, and acceptance.
- Discipline your children with love, wisely balancing freedom with firm boundaries.
- Encourage healthy self-discipline, obedience, and respect for your authority and society's authority; this will translate into conscience, obedience, and respect for God's authority.
- Train your children by demonstrating consistency and predictability so that your child learns to trust and rely upon the parent-child relationship.
- Give your children guidance, but also give them opportunities to make their own decisions, to make their own mistakes, and to take responsibility for their own choices.
- Teach your children about the deceptions and attractive perils of the world.
- Prepare your children to make a conscious, considered decision to accept Jesus Christ as their Lord and personal Savior.
- Accurately and faithfully model God's true image to your children in your words and actions.
- Teach the stories, principles, and promises of God to your children, engraving them into your children's hearts and minds through repetition and example, as the Lord commands us so clearly in Deuteronomy 11:18–21:

> Fix these words of mine in your hearts and minds; tie them as symbols on your hands and bind them on your foreheads. Teach them to your children, talking about them when you sit at home and when you walk along the road, when you lie down and when you get up. Write them on the doorframes of your houses and on your gates, so that your days and the days of your children may be many in the land that the LORD swore to give your forefathers, as many as the days that the heavens are above the earth.

"What's More Important?"

THE COACH GIVES MICHAEL a lift home. As Michael gets out of the car, the coach pats Michael on the back and says, "Great game, great effort. You should be proud, son."

Michael doesn't feel proud—and that word *son* makes him wince inside. His own father should have been there, giving him that pat on the back, saying those words to him.

But his father doesn't show up at home until almost an hour later. Michael is in the den watching TV when his dad comes in.

"I stopped by the school, but no one was there," says J. W. Brown, settling into his recliner and unfolding his newspaper. "Game over so soon?"

Michael shrugs.

"Who won?" J. W. asks absently, his tone of voice indicating that he is paying more attention to his newspaper than to his son.

"We did," says Michael. "I hit a home run."

"Oh? Good for you."

"The last run. It won the game."

J. W. turns a page and continues reading his paper. "That's great, Son."

Michael leans toward his father, grabs a corner of the newspaper, and shakes it to get J. W.'s attention. "Dad," Michael says insistently, "you were supposed to be there for the first pitch."

J. W. looks up in annoyance, pulling his newspaper out of Michael's reach. "Stop that," he says. "What are you talking about?"

"You promised, Dad. You said you'd be at the game."

J. W.'s eyes narrow. "Look, Son, I'm sorry I missed your game, but something important came up after the committee meeting. Pastor Knight asked me to stay for a planning session for the new sanctuary fund drive."

"But you *promised!*"

"I know I promised, but sometimes plans change, and kids just have to accept that."

"So kids have to keep their promises, but parents don't?"

"Look, Son," J. W. says gruffly, "I don't want to hear any more about this, understand? You're being very selfish about this. After all, which is more important? God's work—or a kid's baseball game?" He snaps his paper and hides behind it.

Michael will remember his dad's words—and the feeling of worthlessness they've hammered into him—for the rest of his life.

Five Principles for Spiritual Growth

HERE ARE FIVE PRACTICAL, biblical principles to remember in all ages and stages of your child's psychological, emotional, and spiritual development.

Principle One: Your Child's Spiritual Growth Takes Place in an Orderly Progression of Stages

Each stage is a platform for the next stage. The continued development of your child's spiritual growth depends in large part on how successfully he completes the tasks of the previous stage. It should not surprise us that these stages are so orderly, because they were designed by God, who is a God of order, not a God of confusion. He has ordained specific laws of creation that are appropriate to facilitate all human growth, including physical, emotional, mental, social, and spiritual growth.

What children learn about God and spirituality at one stage prepares them for what they will learn at the next stage. What they have learned at these two stages prepares them for what they will learn at the next stage, as we see in the diagram below.

Stages of Spiritual Development

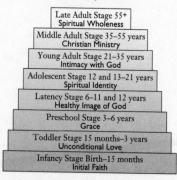

Late Adult Stage 55+
Spiritual Wholeness

Middle Adult Stage 35–55 years
Christian Ministry

Young Adult Stage 21–35 years
Intimacy with God

Adolescent Stage 12 and 13–21 years
Spiritual Identity

Latency Stage 6–11 and 12 years
Healthy Image of God

Preschool Stage 3–6 years
Grace

Toddler Stage 15 months–3 years
Unconditional Love

Infancy Stage Birth–15 months
Initial Faith

Principle Two: Timing Is Everything

In some areas of life, we can take shortcuts and everything still turns out okay—but not in this area. In spiritual growth, developmental tasks must be completed at certain times. If a child fails to successfully complete a given developmental task, he doesn't simply fail to advance—he moves along the wrong path. If he fails to complete the task of developing trust, he sinks into mistrust; if he fails to achieve autonomy, he sinks into shame and self-doubt. If a child is not moving forward developmentally, emotionally, psychologically, and spiritually, he is moving backward.

Principle Three: Emotional Development Has a Powerful Influence on Spiritual Development

The diagram below shows how the stages of personality growth coincide with the stages of spiritual growth.

For example, if you look at the bottom of the two pyramids, you can see that at the same time an individual is trying to learn how to trust, the person is also developing faith. Further up the pyramid, as an individual is attempting to learn to experience intimacy with others, the person is also learning how to experience a level of closeness or intimacy with God.

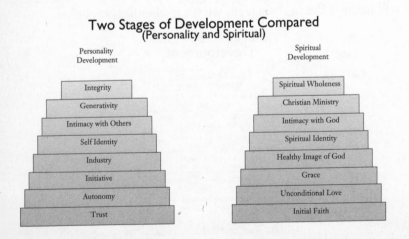

Two Stages of Development Compared
(Personality and Spiritual)

Personality Development	Spiritual Development
Integrity	Spiritual Wholeness
Generativity	Christian Ministry
Intimacy with Others	Intimacy with God
Self Identity	Spiritual Identity
Industry	Healthy Image of God
Initiative	Grace
Autonomy	Unconditional Love
Trust	Initial Faith

If we put the two developmental models together, as below, we arrive at a model of spiritual growth integrating the two distinct developmental paths.

The darker floors of the foundation represent the various personality stages that one goes through, while the lighter floors represent the spiritual foundations that are laid throughout one's life. Here you see how one's personality development undergirds one's spiritual development.

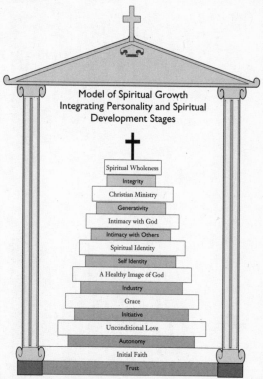

Model of Spiritual Growth
Integrating Personality and Spiritual
Development Stages

Spiritual Wholeness
Integrity
Christian Ministry
Generativity
Intimacy with God
Intimacy with Others
Spiritual Identity
Self Identity
A Healthy Image of God
Industry
Grace
Initiative
Unconditional Love
Autonomy
Initial Faith
Trust

Principle Four: Failure in Emotional Development Almost Insures Failure in Spiritual Development

We see this principle illustrated in the diagram on page 136. This diagram compares two spiritual development structures. On the left, we see a model of healthy spiritual development. All the personality and emotional foundations have been adequately

A Comparison of Two Spiritual Development Paths: Secure and Insecure

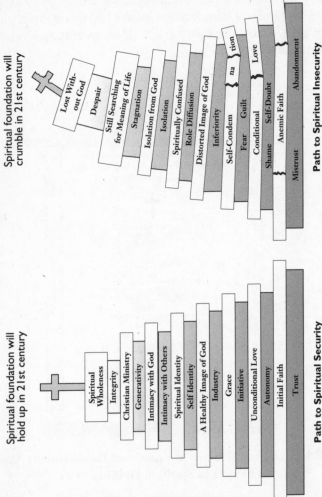

Spiritual foundation will hold up in 21st century

- Spiritual Wholeness
- Integrity
- Christian Ministry
- Generativity
- Intimacy with God
- Intimacy with Others
- Spiritual Identity
- Self Identity
- A Healthy Image of God
- Industry
- Grace
- Initiative
- Unconditional Love
- Autonomy
- Initial Faith
- Trust

Path to Spiritual Security
Healthy and Mature Emotional Foundation

Spiritual foundation will crumble in 21st century

- Lost Without God
- Despair
- Still Searching for Meaning of Life
- Stagnation
- Isolation from God
- Isolation
- Spiritually Confused
- Role Diffusion
- Distorted Image of God
- Inferiority
- Self-Condemnation
- Fear Guilt
- Conditional Love
- Shame Self-Doubt
- Anemic Faith
- Mistrust
- Abandonment

Path to Spiritual Insecurity
Unhealthy and Immature Emotional Foundation

laid, providing adequate support for this individual's spiritual growth throughout life.

On the right, we see the damage that results from the failure to successfully negotiate various levels of personality and emotional development. If you look closely at the bottom of the unhealthy model on the right, you can see that this individual has no emotional capacity to trust. In fact, this person has learned to mistrust, and the result is a flawed, cracked spiritual foundation of anemic faith. Failure at this earliest stage of development has a ripple effect throughout this individual's life.

If you are fortunate enough to have the opportunity, do not wait until your child is an adolescent or an adult to start being a better parent or a better Christian. You can't wait until later to start "fixing" your child's personality and spirituality. To raise a spiritually secure child, start now, right where you are, right where your child is. Once the damage has been done in a child's spiritual or emotional life, it is difficult to break into the personality or spiritual development structure and correct major developmental flaws—much as it would be difficult to repair a broken foundation once a house has been built on top of it.

If damage has already been done, of course, the situation is certainly not hopeless. By God's healing grace and with the help of professional Christian counseling, the broken foundations of personality and spirituality can be repaired—but that takes a lot of work. If problems can be solved at an earlier stage of development, the healing and repair process is much easier.

Principle Five: God's Provision for the Spiritual Growth Potential Within Your Child Is Found in You

Because you are the child's only early source of spiritual growth and nurture, you occupy a strategic position in the child's life. Your influence will either enhance or impede future spiritual development. The way you meet your child's early spiritual needs will tend to either draw your child toward Christ—or push your child away from Christ. The emotional and spiritual environment you create around your child largely determines the outcome of your child's life, both in this world and in the world to come.

How precious is your child to God? In Matthew 18:10–14, Jesus tells a story to answer that question—the story of a man who had a flock of a hundred sheep. When one of the hundred went astray and became lost, the man left the flock and searched everywhere until he found the lost sheep. Jesus expects no less of us, the parents who care for his little children, his lambs. As shepherds of little lambs, we need to understand the needs of the lambs, because lambs cannot tell you what their needs are. We need to understand that the childhood years are crucial to the spiritual growth of a child and that each stage has its own pattern, its own needs. The better we understand those stages, the better we can meet the needs of our children—and the better their experience of God and faith will be.

"Train up a child in the way he should go," says Proverbs 22:6 (KJV), "and when he is old, he will not depart from it." As parents, we are commanded to be not only good Christians but also good shepherds of God's lambs, good baby-sitters for his precious children.

EIGHT

Practical Steps to Securing Your Child's Spiritual Growth

TEARS ROLLED DOWN HANNA'S cheeks as she cuddled and cradled her six-year-old daughter, Jenea. The little girl reached up to her mother's face and touched a teardrop, holding it up on her fingertip, like a jewel. "Why are you crying, Mommy?" asked Jenea.

"Because I'm so happy, sweetheart."

"You cry when you're happy, Mommy?" the girl asked with a quizzical expression.

"Sometimes."

"I only cry when I'm sad."

"Someday, sweetheart," said Hanna, "you'll know what it feels like to be so happy that the happiness just has to squeeze right out of you." She kissed her daughter's puzzled face and smiled.

"It squeezes out of you in teardrops, Mommy?"

"That's right."

Jenea pondered this concept in silence for a minute or so. Then she said, "I don't know if I *ever* want to be *that* happy."

"Of course you do, sweetie."

"Are you happy because of what I did today?"

"Yes. That's why I'm so happy."

"Then I'm gonna do it again. I'm gonna do it every day. Just to make you happy."

"You only have to do it once, sweetheart," said Hanna, "and it lasts forever and ever and ever. When you ask Jesus to come into your heart, he comes in and he lives inside you and he never, ever goes away."

"And I get to go to heaven?"

"And you get to go to heaven."

"Thank you, Mommy."

"For what?"

"For telling me how to ask Jesus into my heart. 'Cause you know what? I think I'm so happy, I'm crying too!"

Spiritual Growth Curves: Infancy Through Preschool

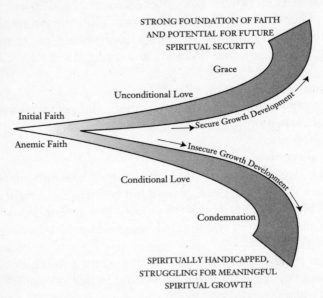

Secure and Insecure Spiritual Growth Curves
(Infancy through Preschool 0–6 years old)

STRONG FOUNDATION OF FAITH
AND POTENTIAL FOR FUTURE
SPIRITUAL SECURITY

Grace

Unconditional Love

Initial Faith

Secure Growth Development

Anemic Faith

Insecure Growth Development

Conditional Love

Condemnation

SPIRITUALLY HANDICAPPED,
STRUGGLING FOR MEANINGFUL
SPIRITUAL GROWTH

The above diagram relates to the first three stages of spiritual growth that your child must complete, or, in some cases, fail. The upward curve represents your child's path to spiritual security. By spiritually secure I mean that a child's faith remains strong and meaningful through life, and that he is able to live the Spirit-filled life throughout the course of his life. For a child to be able to achieve a strong potential for future spiritual security during ado-lescence and adulthood, he will have to achieve the spiritual growth of stages of initial faith, unconditional love, and grace.

Just as with the life development curves discussed earlier, which dealt with personality and emotional development, failure to adequately complete these first three stages of spiritual growth results in a downward direction in a child's long-term spiritual growth. The downward curve represents the path to spiritual insecurity that a child may end up taking if he fails to achieve these early stages. A spiritually insecure child grows up without the abil-ity to consistently experience the joy, peace, and strength of his faith throughout life's trials. Instead, he experiences a life reigned by fear, worry, and uncertainty. The end result of the child trav-eling down the path of spiritual insecurity is a weak or collapsed spiritual foundation, leaving the child in a position of being poten-tially spiritually handicapped, struggling for future meaningful spiritual growth for the years to come.

On the other hand, you can clearly see the positive results even at six years of age for a child who travels the secure path. This six-year-old, whether he realizes it or not, already possesses a strong foundation of faith and potential for future spiritual secu-rity. His faith foundation may be called strong because it is, first, experiential. When this child becomes an adolescent or adult, what he reads in the Bible about God and the Christian life will be real and meaningful, not just token words on a page. Why? Because what he comes to believe about God throughout life matches what he experienced in real life while growing up.

As parents, it is important to consider the infancy, toddler, and preschool stages of personality and emotional development as the main sources of support for your child's early and later stages of spiritual growth.

Infancy Stage: Initial Faith vs. Anemic Faith

Jenea was born into a Christian home. From the time she was an infant, she has been experiencing spiritual needs and spiritual growth appropriate to her stage in life. Now, at the tender age of six, she has reached a point of decision making in her spiritual experience. Though she is far too young to understand all of the ramifications of her choice, she is developmentally ready to decide to follow Jesus and to ask him to come into her life in a powerful way.

Jenea's decision didn't take place in a vacuum. It was preceded by many small steps of preparation as Hanna and Scott guided and nurtured her spiritual development. Oh, they made some mistakes, to be sure. But Hanna was determined not to recycle the parenting style of her father, no matter how well intentioned he might have been. Instead, she decided to break the cycle of unhealthy religious traditions in her family. She decided to meet her daughter's emotional and relational needs from birth to young adulthood. In this way, Hanna carefully built a strong foundation for her daughter's spiritual growth, beginning in the very first weeks of Jenea's life.

The key foundation and primary task of the infancy stage of spiritual growth are listed below:

Spiritual Foundation Stone: Developing initial faith

Primary Task: Develops capacity to internalize God as an object of security and trust

The initial foundation stone for spiritual growth is built in the first fifteen months of life. Whether this foundation is sound and solid or cracked and crumbling is almost exclusively in the hands of the parents. Here we see the spiritual qualities that Christian parents should seek to encourage in the infancy stage of life to ensure that the infant's primary task is completed.

Since the infant child cannot understand the concept of God at this stage of mental development, you—the parent—represent God to the child. If you, as the God-figure, enable your child to feel loved and secure, then you will build a firm foundation for your child to grow up experiencing God as a source of love and security. Your child will be able to build on this spiritual foundation, growing in such beliefs as "God is love," "God loves me," "I can trust God," and "I love God." Here are some specific ways you can build and strengthen the spiritual foundation of the infancy stage.

Communicate with your child through his senses. Because your child experiences the world through the senses, it is important that you do lots of cooing and cuddling with your child and use eye communication to convey a personal connection with him.

Meet your child's physical needs. The child's physical needs translate to emotional needs. When you meet those needs for warmth, comfort, food, and holding, you are meeting his emotional needs.

Be consistent with your infant. Repeat the words, sounds, touches, and nurturing again and again, whenever you are with the child. Consistency gives him the sense of security that comes with familiarity.

Be available. Be there when your infant needs you—not when it is convenient or when a commercial is on TV. The child is in an egocentric stage. It may not seem reasonable to you to be at the beck and call of an infant, but God designed that infant to base his trust in you (and ultimately his trust in God) on the fact that you are instantly available when that child needs you.

Be patient. Stay with your infant as long as he needs you. Empathize with his feelings and needs. Base the time you spend nurturing your child on his need for you, not on your need for him. This may (and usually does) mean that you should spend several hours a day just holding and communicating with your child, as a positive contribution to his emotional and spiritual development.

Be the primary caregiver in your child's experience. This is especially true if you are the mother, but it is also true for fathers. Your child bonds with his primary caregiver and needs to consistently know you are there. Your child cannot bond with a stream of different people passing through his life, nor should he at this stage be emotionally bonding with the maid, the au pair, Aunt Mary, or even grandma and grandpa. Grandparents are important individuals in your child's life, and visits and holding by grandparents and other relatives is certainly OK, but in the first fifteen months of life, a child needs to feel the consistent warmth and nurturing of his parents—primarily from mom and secondarily from dad.

If your child has too many "people objects" to internalize in a short period of time, he may become confused about who he can trust. This confusion may, in some cases, lead to the beginnings of neurotic fear and anxiety. This is not to say that mothers should feel guilty when they are forced by circumstances of single parenthood or economic necessity to work outside the home and leave their children in day care situations. I would, however, suggest that mothers in that situation carefully consider whether they truly need to work outside the home; if any alternative can be found so that mom can stay home with the child, that alternative is certainly preferable, for the sake of the emotional and spiritual development of the child (at least until the child is older). If mom must work outside the home, she should provide consistency in caregiving—for example, a grandparent or a highly trusted hired individual who will spend time on a consistent, long-term basis, modeling God's love, nurturing, and security to that child.

An infant who is deprived of the kind of consistent, available, patient care I just described grows up emotionally handicapped—and an emotional handicap tends to produce spiritual handicaps. If the child learns to expect inconsistent, unreliable, unavailable, neglectful care from his parents during the first fifteen months of life, he will grow to expect such negative treatment from God as well. He will conclude that he cannot depend on God or anyone else for the love and care that he needs throughout his life.

When you, as a loving Christian parent, provide your infant with the time and experiences that enable him to internalize you as an object of love and security, you establish the capacity for trust that will form the nucleus of genuine spiritual faith. This capacity for trust is the foundation upon which your child will build the next stage of his spiritual growth.

Toddler Stage: Unconditional Love vs. Conditional Love

During the infancy stage of spiritual growth which we just discussed, your child may be considered spiritually helpless in that he completely depends on you for spiritual nourishment. However, his tiny human spirit contains an innate drive to seek, to know, and to experience God. This spiritual drive can continue to flourish only to the degree that you understand and meet his spiritual needs as a two- to three-year-old. If your toddler is not aware of his needs for spiritual growth and cannot communicate them to you, how will they be met? Meeting your child's spiritual needs during toddlerhood involves several key ingredients.

Spiritual Foundation Stone: Internalizing God's unconditional love

Primary Task: Experiences God's forgiveness, unconditional love, and acceptance through parents while becoming an autonomous, separate individual

- Child must begin to gain a sense of who he is as an autonomous, separate individual while maintaining an emotional lifeline of dependence upon parents
- Child experiences forgiveness, unconditional love, and acceptance so that he can be affirmed and feel OK as an autonomous, separate individual

During this stage, an important foundational stone is laid that greatly affects the direction of the child's future spiritual growth and faith in God. If your toddler can internalize God's unconditional love (feel that he is lovable and worthwhile to you even while experiencing inner frustrations with your loving authority), he will be more likely to accept the fact that God—the greatest authority figure of all—can love and accept him, too.

The emotional foundation that must be laid in toddlerhood is threefold: (1) identity and autonomy; (2) positive self-esteem; and (3) positive attitude toward authority and learning. Here are the practical steps you can take to help your child build this threefold foundation.

Stay above the fray. The toddler stage is rife with conflict—both conflict within the child's own emotions, and conflict between the child and his parents. Though he needs love and limits, he also demands complete physical freedom and is intolerant when his immediate wants are frustrated. He doesn't want to be dependent on you or anyone else; he wants to do everything himself—and this is perfectly normal and natural. It is part of his God-given drive to set himself apart as an individual. Avoid taking the toddler's frustration, independence, or conflict personally; react on an adult level, not the child's level. Stay above the fray. If you trade anger for anger, frustration for frustration, you will evoke shame and low self-worth in the child.

Communicate unconditional love to your child. Whatever his negative behavior or feelings, let your child know he is accepted and wanted. In order for a child to grow up sensing God's unconditional love in his life, he must sense your unconditional love when he is a toddler. He must have the experience of being accepted and forgiven even while he is being disciplined and instructed.

Know when to control and when to let go. Have a good balance of yes's and no's. Provide an appropriate mixture of freedom and consistent, appropriate controls and boundaries. Try to find ways to say yes as much as possible. For example, instead of saying, "No, you can't watch Bert and Ernie now; you have to take a nap," say, "Yes, you can watch Bert and Ernie, right after you get up from your nap." By helping the child to feel he lives in an environment of freedom and independence, a yes environment, you help him feel more positive about himself, his life, his parents, and God, even when his wants are sometimes frustrated or denied. Continually controlling a child and telling him no—especially if there is also yelling and shaming—tends to embitter the child and give him a negative outlook on self, life, parents, and God.

Major on the majors, not the minors. Many parents make major issues over minor problems, imposing perfectionist expectations on their children. This kind of legalistic parenting leads either to embittered children who reject the faith of their parents or legalistic children who repeat the errors of their parents in the next generation. Even at the toddler stage, children should be learning lessons about the grace and mercy of God. By being flexible rather than rigid in parenting your child, you express the freedom of God's grace to him, instead of the bondage of the law.

Pray with your toddler. You would be amazed at how early in life a child can understand the meaning and importance of prayer. In her book *The Spiritual Needs of Children*, Judith Shelly tells the story of a two-year-old named Amy. One night while her parents were away and she was being cared for by a baby-sitter, little Amy stood in her crib, shrieking, "Pay! Pay!" The baby-sitter tried to understand what was causing the toddler so much distress. She reviewed the notes Amy's parents had left on how to care for Amy—"brush teeth, potty, pajamas, drink, Bible story, good-night kiss, Raggedy Ann, favorite blanket, tuck her in, turn off the light, leave the door ajar." There was nothing in the note about "pay."

Still, Amy continued crying out, "Pay! Pay!" Finally it dawned on the baby-sitter: Amy wanted to *pray!* She sat down by Amy's crib, folded her hands, and said a simple prayer. Little Amy quieted down, folded her hands, and bowed her head. Then when the baby-sitter said, "Amen," Amy settled down onto the mattress, snuggled up to Raggedy Ann, and soon went to sleep. Even at the age of two, this little girl was able to experience the beginnings of an intimate relationship with God.

Take stock of your child's spiritual perceptions. Children form impressions of God through the way we interact with them, and it is important that we discover what kinds of impressions they are forming. Do they experience God as warm, sensitive, caring, and loving? Or do they perceive him as cold, noncaring, and judgmental?

One way to take stock of a child's spiritual perceptions is by inviting him to draw a picture of God. One three-year-old who was asked to draw God drew a human form surrounded by a colorful assortment of circles, squares, and triangles. She explained, "It's a person and my mommy giving me a kiss. My mommy loves God." This is a child whose parents are providing a healthy, experiential model of a loving God. Another child drew God as a large figure hovering over three human figures. The child explained, "God is going to get mad, because no one is good." This child's perception of an angry, judgmental God has likely been influenced by angry, critical parenting.

If, after taking stock of your toddler's perception of God, you find that you have been conveying a distorted image of God to your child, then immediately begin to take steps to better model the character of God to your child, by being more loving, patient, merciful, accepting, forgiving, and affirming. If you have difficulty demonstrating these qualities of the character of God—if, for example, you have strong tendencies toward legalism, perfection-ism, being hypercritical, exhibiting rage or uncontrollable anger, being abusive or neglectful—then seek professional counseling to overcome these tendencies so that the next time your child draws a picture of God, it is a picture of joy, love, and happiness.

———

Easter Sunday—Jenea's spiritual birthday

It all started with the children's sermon in church this morning. The minister called all the children to the front of the church. He had a paper bag in his hand, and he pulled things out of it—first a flower, then a toy pistol. He made some application of these items to the Resurrection, saying they were like the cross of Jesus. I don't blame the kids for being confused by this object lesson, because even I couldn't figure it out!

When Jenea came home and asked me to explain the chil-dren's sermon to her, I told her I didn't get it, either. But then we got to talking about Easter and Jesus, and one thing led to another. I ended up telling her the plan of salvation, and Jenea said, "I want to do that, too. I want Jesus to live in my heart."

I said, "Do you want to pray to Jesus right now and ask him into your heart?"

And she said, "Okay, but I'll pray silently and say, 'Amen' when I'm done."

I said, "All right," then I silently prayed for her while she prayed. Afterward I asked Jenea what she prayed, and she said she prayed that Jesus would live inside her and also that God would forgive all her sins. She seemed to really understand what she was doing—exactly as a little child should understand.

It was the most beautiful experience I've ever known.

Preschool Stage: Grace vs. Self-Condemnation

As parents of a preschooler, you will begin to see not only your child's emotional growth, but his spiritual growth taking off like a rocket. Since your three- to five-year-old is more emotion-ally sensitive and more intellectually curious at this age, the atten-tion required by your child to his spiritual needs will be great. At this age your child still doesn't have a realization of his spiritual needs to the point that he is self-motivated or able to meet them on his own. Let's now explore this crucial and intricate period of your child's spiritual growth.

Spiritual Foundation Stone: Internalizing God's grace

Primary Tasks: (1) Continues to believe and trust God's uncon-ditional love and acceptance, (2) learns to trust God for forgive-ness, (3) begins to see God's world as good, and (4) develops positive early spiritual concepts

As a preschooler, your child begins to gain a grasp of such concepts as love, parents, givers, and helpers. Positive experiences with parents mold the child's positive image of God. Concepts such as "God is love," "God is good," "God is a Father," and so forth become easier for a child who has received positive experi-ences from his primary caregivers from infancy through this stage. That child is now prepared to begin applying the truth of the Bible to his life.

How much spiritual information can a child absorb at the preschool stage? More, perhaps, than you might realize. Here are some of the basic spiritual concepts that your preschool child can and should develop at this stage.

God. God is love. God loves me. God loves, accepts, and for-gives children. God is a just authority figure who judges right and wrong, but he is also a merciful Father who forgives us when we turn to him. God, the Creator, made the world. God, the Cre-ator, made me and has chosen me to be one of his children.

God is real. God is perfect. God can create life. God commu-nicates with us. God wants us to respect him, ourselves, and others.

Forgiveness. No matter how bad our mistakes are, nothing is too bad for God to forgive. If we are really sorry for our mistakes, God will forgive us. If we accept God's forgiveness, we do not have to feel guilty or bad about ourselves.

Jesus. Jesus is God. Jesus is also a person like us, though he never sinned. Jesus lived so that you and I can understand God better and so that we can learn how God wants us to live. Jesus died to take away our sins. Jesus rose from the dead, because God has power over death. Because Jesus is alive today, we will be alive forever, even after we die.

Holy Spirit. The Holy Spirit is God in the world today. The Holy Spirit lives in us when we invite Jesus into our hearts. The Spirit comforts us and guides us and talks to us through our conscience, showing us the difference between right and wrong.

The Bible. The Bible is God's message to us, and God's message is true. By listening to God's Word, we learn how God wants us to live, and we learn of God's love for us.

The Church. The church is made of people all around the world who love and follow Jesus. The church is not a building; it is people. God wants all of his followers to come together on a regular basis to worship him, learn about him, serve him, and care for each other. God wants his followers to love each other and help each other and tell others about him, so that more and more people will become followers of Jesus, too.

People. Each person is unique, special, and created by God for a special purpose. Every one of us has abilities God can use. Every one of us needs God. We all have the freedom to make good decisions or bad decisions; bad decisions are called sin, and they hurt us and make us unhappy. When we make good decisions that please God, those decisions make us happy and make God happy. We all sin, we all make bad decisions, but if we ask God every day to help us make good decisions, we can do good things and make God, ourselves, and other people very happy.

Heaven. Heaven is being with God forever.

Hell. Hell is being separated from God forever. (Avoid scaring a child into a relationship with God by giving lurid descriptions of hell. When Jesus dealt with children, he attracted them with his love. He directed his "fire and brimstone" sermons to adults who were smug and complacent, such as the Pharisees and the rich who ignored the plight of the poor.)

The devil. The devil is God's enemy.

Sin. Sin is disobeying God.

At this stage, the child is a ball of powerful feelings, and he needs you to: (1) accept him, even with his negative behavior and feelings; (2) help him find constructive ways to express and deal with his negative feelings; and (3) direct him appropriately before he loses control. Despite your child's drive for independence, he remains very much dependent on you and needs to know that you and God still provide for him, protect him, want him, love him, and forgive him. These are the roots your child needs for you to lay down for him as he begins to internalize the concept of God's grace.

Emotional and spiritual growth coincide profoundly at this delicate time of foundation laying. The child is in the fantasy stage and unable to completely separate fantasy from reality. He does not think like an adult. The child learns through repetition, so you must repeatedly teach and demonstrate unconditional love to him, even through times of negative behavior. He needs your consistency in discipline and forgiveness so that he can internalize you as a positive object of self-discipline and self-control, which leads to the formation of conscience and a sense of God's directing presence. Some practical suggestions to help you guide your child's development through the crucial preschool years are provided below.

When the child becomes angry, respond calmly. Focus on helping and directing your child rather than scolding or shaming him. The normal human tendency when a child yells is to yell back even louder in order to be heard over the noise. Instead, try speaking very softly. The child will have to quiet down to hear what you are saying, and children often adjust their own tone and behavior to the tone their parents use. Softening your tone often softens theirs. If the child is out of control, use a "time-out," placing the child in a chair or on a bed to give him an opportunity to bring his feelings under control. "I'll talk to you about it," you may calmly, reasonably say, "when you stop yelling and talk sweetly." Be consistent, repeat the message calmly, and wait until the child is ready to respond in a controlled way. This response shows the child that you will not be provoked to anger (which is a way children often try to control their parents), and it shows them that tantrums and outrageous behavior do not work.

Give your child a lot of approval. Both verbally through praise and affirmation, and physically through hugs and pats on the back. This will provide your child with incentives for achievement, and motivation to learn and grow.

Be open and accepting. Make sure your child knows that he can come to you with any problem, failure, sin, or confession and you will always hear him, love him, forgive him, and accept him as a good and worthy person. Make sure he knows that sins and mistakes don't make him a bad person and that everyone fails from time to time. Let him know that you want to help him recover and move forward, not shame him or beat him down. When your child experiences consistent grace and forgiveness, he will be consistent in confessing and repenting from sins and mistakes, and will be more likely to make godly choices in the future.

Your goal during this stage of your preschooler's development is to teach him to respond to you out of love and respect, not just out of fear of punishment. You are attempting to build an authentic working conscience into your child, not just a punishment-avoidance mechanism. In matters of sin and disobedience, seek to deal with him out of love, conveying to him that everything you do (even the things that are unpleasant to him) are done because you want the best for him, not because you are mad at him. If you are careful not to frustrate your preschooler's need for unconditional love, approval, acceptance, self-esteem, and grace, you will open the door for your child to experience genuine spiritual security and to understand key spiritual concepts such as forgiveness and grace. These concepts will not be mere theological terms to him; they will be experiences he has been immersed in since childhood.

Work with your spouse to be good models of God's character in the home. Avoid angry outbursts and open conflict with your spouse. If there are problems in the marriage, seek counseling so that they can be managed in a healthy way. By creating a healthy home environment for your child, you instill in him a positive attitude about life and family. He will grow to feel good about the concept of parenthood (including that of his heavenly Parent). He will grow to love, honor, and respect you, and he will want to imitate you; ultimately he will be able to love, honor, and respect God as his heavenly Parent and as the ultimate example he wants to imitate for life.

Use the repetition of rituals to teach your child about God. Involve your child in the three basic rituals of Bible reading, prayer, and church attendance. Prayer should be natural, uncomplicated, informal talking with God. Avoid words that create distance between your child and God—strange, foreign words such as King James English. When Jesus prayed to the Father, he didn't say "thee" and "thou" in his own language. He called God "Abba," which was the Aramaic version of "Daddy" or "Da-Da." He addressed God in simple, childlike terms, and that is how we should teach our children to relate to their "heavenly Da-Da." Keep prayers short, personal, and practical: "Please help Jordan not to be afraid of visiting the dentist" or, "Please help Erica find her missing library book."

Make time for regular, daily family devotions in the home. Use children's Bible-story books and children's songs to teach and reinforce spiritual principles that you exemplify by your life. Let your children hear you praying for them, thanking God for them and praying for their future. Let them hear you address God as a loving heavenly Father who gives good gifts. Pray specifically for your child's hurts, needs, and fears, no matter how trivial they seem from an adult perspective. Remember how large those issues loom in the minds and emotions of children.

When teaching spiritual concepts to your child, focus on daily experience rather than facts and memorization. Many children can rattle off facts or verses but have little idea what they mean. Children need to understand how to practice the Christian basics— obedience, forgiveness, prayer, love—in their everyday lives.

When teaching about God, focus on Jesus. According to experts, children at about the ages of two to six are concrete thinkers. They view God as if he is a man; physical characteristics tend to predominate the God images of a child at this age. Drawings by preschoolers often show God wearing pants and a shirt, with hands, feet, and a beard, and show him eating or drinking something. Some preschool children may point to the pastor and say, "Mommy, there's God." Children also point to pictures of people in Bible-story books and ask, "Is that God?" For this reason, it is often helpful to point the child to Jesus, "the Word made flesh," because they can identify with his birth as a baby and with his humanity.

Use stories to convey Christian truth and meaningful lessons. Preschool children love Bible stories, especially those with plenty of action. Through stories, they can begin to understand that God loves them and that he created them. Tell Bible stories in your own words or use appropriate paraphrased versions of biblical stories, written at a child's level. Use Christian books about contemporary children in contemporary situations that illustrate timeless truths about God that your child can understand. Explain the meaning of Bible stories in terms they can understand, and select stories featuring children they can identify with. Be alert to misconceptions your children might gain from a story heard at Sunday school or at home.

Some well-meaning parents and teachers do harm to their children's image of God by reading from the King James Version and not explaining what the Shakespearean words mean. It is a major mistake to teach the Sesame Street generation from the seventeenth-century translation. After all, what mental image arises in the mind of today's child when he hears Jesus say, "Suffer the little children"?

When teaching preschoolers, avoid verbal, intellectual methods; use experiential, fun, playful methods. Sermons and even object lessons go over a preschooler's head. Preschoolers learn most by doing and least by listening. Use play (a toy Noah's ark or nativity scene, drawing pictures of Bible stories, modeling Bible events with clay) to engage a child's interest and communicate life principles. Do not complicate the Christian faith with theological concepts or historical facts that children cannot assimilate; keep it simple.

Take advantage of "teachable moments." Use events in the child's life as opportunities for relating Bible principles to real-life situations. If your child is too short to see the parade and must be lifted onto your shoulders, remind him of the time Zaccheaus needed to climb a tree to see Jesus. If your two children are arguing over who should be first in line for a privilege, remind them of the time the disciples argued over who should be first in Jesus' kingdom and he taught them that they were to serve one another. When at the beach or the miniature golf course or at the park, take a moment with your child to thank God for fun, for sunlight, and for his beautiful world that is ours to enjoy. Don't miss everyday opportunities to teach your child how to experience God.

Practice what you preach. Whatever you teach your child, make sure you are also living it out in your own life. If you adopt a teaching philosophy of "do as I say, not as I do," you will cancel out with your actions every lesson you try to teach. Your actions always speak louder than your words.

Invite your child to imitate your life. Show your child the good, Christian activities you are involved in, and allow your child to participate or imitate your actions. For example, if you take a bag of clothes or canned goods to the Christian homeless shelter, invite your child to donate some of his things and to go with you and make his donation alongside yours. Explain to him that these donations go to help people who don't have such things and that the people who work at the shelter tell needy people about Jesus.

Accept your child's hard questions. Don't be shocked if your child says, "I don't like God. He could have kept Grandpa well, but he let Grandpa die! Why didn't God help Grandpa?" That is a normal emotion, even for adults. Avoid shaming the child for these normal feelings and questions. Instead, tell the child, "I know how you feel. I miss Grandpa, too, and I wish he could have got well. But God knew that Grandpa would be much happier with him than here on earth. And though it seems as if we'll miss Grandpa for a very long time, it won't be so long before we get to see him and be with him again, in heaven." Be unshockable and accept your child's feelings without condemning or scolding.

Use warm, happy memories to encourage your child's spiritual development. Some of the richest, most lasting memories of our lives are built during our childhood. A child's thinking is more emotional than cognitive, and a child's memory is triggered by strong emotions. A child's memory is more strongly affected by feelings than by facts. Use happy, emotional times to teach spiritual concepts and demonstrate the goodness of God. For example, during a visit to Disneyland, a brief comment can transform a fun experience into a powerfully meaningful experience: "If you think this place is fun, imagine what heaven must be like!" A vacation in the mountains or at the seashore can be used as an object lesson in God's wisdom and creative power. A beautiful sunset or rainbow can be described as a gift of God's love to us.

Make time to be a friend to your child. Read stories to him. Sing with him. Play games with him. Put your grown-up fingers in the modeling clay or finger paints along with him. Make drawings alongside your child, using his crayons and colored markers. Show him that you enjoy his company, and while you are at it, tell your child how Jesus enjoyed playing with children. These activities are beautiful opportunities not merely for teaching spiritual lessons but for making your love relationship with God a natural part of your fun times, your happy moments, and your daily life.

Use eye communication when you talk about God and his love; eye-to-eye contact conveys to your child that you value him and that you enjoy being with him. Early spiritual concepts are received more easily from parents who give their children the gift of their *time* and *attention*.

Use bedtime as a valuable time for teaching spiritual concepts and conveying spiritual experiences. At bedtime your children are eager to cuddle and interact with you. Use those moments to build memories and a sense of trust and security.

Share your spiritual pilgrimage with your child, in terms appropriate to his age and understanding. Talk about the spiritual heritage of father, mother, grandmother, grandfather, and other important people in the family's life. Talk about how you came to know the Lord, how Jesus is a friend to you, and how you talk to God anytime you want to and in any words you want to, not just at meals or at bedtime.

Above all, NEVER USE GOD AS A THREAT! Trying to keep a child in line by telling him that God will hurt him if he sins can destroy a child's image of God for life. I have counseled many people who were threatened this way when they were children; today they see God as an enemy to be feared and even hated. Always portray God as loving, forgiving, and approachable. To use God as a threat is to slander God's character and doom a child's spiritual development.

Spiritual Growth Curves: Latency Through Adolescence

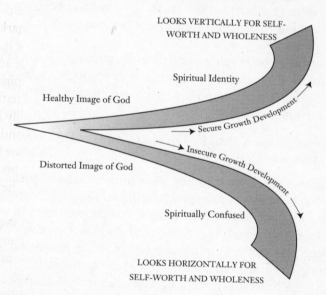

Secure and Insecure Spiritual Growth Curves
(Latency through Adolescence 6–21 years)

LOOKS VERTICALLY FOR SELF-WORTH AND WHOLENESS

Spiritual Identity

Healthy Image of God

Secure Growth Development

Insecure Growth Development

Distorted Image of God

Spiritually Confused

LOOKS HORIZONTALLY FOR SELF-WORTH AND WHOLENESS

The diagram above shows how you can readily see the two spiritual growth paths your child may travel during the latency and adolescent periods of spiritual growth. If your child is spiritually secure when beginning his new journey into latency and adolescence, he will possess the necessary faith to continue along the upward spiritual growth curve. He should be able to easily develop a positive attitude toward God and then learn that he is a child of God and an important part of a spiritual family. The end result of these realizations will be that your adolescent child should be able to look vertically toward God for self-worth and wholeness, not to the secular world at large.

The diagram also clearly demonstrates the dark spiritual path that a six- to twelve-year-old child can fall into if he has failed to achieve the spiritual growth tasks from the previous stages. Instead of seeing God as a positive entity in his life and moving on to see himself as an adopted son into God's family, this child continues to walk down the pathway of spiritual insecurity as someone who fears God and who is confused about his place in God's world. Consequently, for the spiritually insecure adolescent, self-worth and wholeness are not seen as something to be attained in any spiritual sense, but to be met through performance, success, and possession of material things.

In order to be better equipped to be a positive influence in your child's spiritual growth from latency through adolescence, you will need to understand the specifics of your child's spiritual needs during these years.

Latency Stage: A Healthy Image of God vs. a Distorted Image of God

Whether you knew it or not, your primary job as a parent up to now has been one of releasing "spiritual time-release capsules" designed by God to activate at just the right moments in your child's journey through life. Since your child was an infant, you have been planting tiny spiritual seeds in fertile emotional soil, with the goal of one day seeing your child reap a rich spiritual harvest—the harvest of accepting Christ as his personal Savior, of obeying him as Lord, and of following him throughout life and living on with him in eternity. Now, in the latency stage, is when the harvesttime occurs! This next stage of spiritual growth occurs from six to eleven years of age. The primary foundation stone and tasks of this stage are listed below.

Spiritual Foundation Stone: Developing a healthy image of God

Primary Tasks: (1) Sees oneself as a positive spiritual being, (2) develops self-motivation to understand God and learn about spiritual concepts, (3) learns to trust God for guidance and support, (4) learns to enjoy spiritual experiences such as worship, prayer, and devotions, (5) begins to love and serve others voluntarily, and (6) begins an individual, personal relationship with God

Because of the work you did in meeting your child's spiritual and emotional needs from infancy to preschool, your child is now emotionally and spiritually prepared to accomplish the task of knowing God personally by choice. The primary spiritual foundation stone of latency is for the child to see God positively and more clearly—so that he will be attracted to God for a lifetime. This means that the child must develop a healthy image of God.

Our image of God is based in large part on what we are taught as children in church, Sunday school, Christian school, as well as what is taught and modeled in the home. Our early instruction can have both positive and negative effects on our image of God, as the story of Martha illustrates.

When Martha came to me for counseling, she was thirty years old and very troubled in her relationship with God. "You'd think the daughter of a seminary professor would have it all together spiritually," she said. "That's why I feel so guilty. I've had all the advantages of a Christian home—no, a *super*-Christian home, an *ultra*-Christian home. My dad, after all, is a professional Christian. He makes his living being a Christian. Yet here I am, doubting that God loves me, that God even exists."

As I counseled Martha, the sources of her spiritual problems soon became apparent. "My dad always told us, 'God's judgment is sure and swift,'" she told me during our third session together. "And, 'Be sure, your sins will find you out'—that was one of my dad's favorite sayings. I grew up in constant terror of a demanding, perfectionistic God. I was always walking on eggshells around God—crunch, crunch, crunch with my big, clumsy, sinful galoshes! I always wondered, 'What if I believe the wrong things about God or salvation? What if I misinterpret the Bible? Maybe God will send me to hell for having the wrong doctrine—and I'll never even know what I did wrong!' I even pictured God *allowing* me to make mistakes because he *wanted* to punish me! I grew up scared of God and afraid to even read my Bible. The more I feared God, the less I wanted to find out about him."

Unfortunately, Martha's experience is all too common among people raised in religious homes. While *positive* Christian teaching and experiences can enable children to grow up with a very close, bonded relationship with God, *negative* religious teaching and experiences can sometimes be more destructive than no religious teaching at all! At least people from non-Christian, nonreligious homes who encounter Jesus Christ later in life don't have a lot of negative religious baggage to unpack (such as Martha's false image of God as a cruel cosmic enemy eager for a chance to trip people up and send them to hell).

Of all the people I have counseled, the most tragic cases have been those exposed to religious legalism in early life, as Martha was. People from legalistic homes tend to have the most distorted images of God, and the greatest struggles with toxic emotions of shame, anger, fear, and anxiety. They are unable to experience the full range of God's relational personality—his mercy, love, compassion, and empathy. They live in a spiritual and emotional prison of bondage and guilt.

As I have counseled Martha, I have seen a gradual change in her. She is beginning to see the God of the Bible in a different light—not as a demanding perfectionist but as a patient, loving, accepting Father, full of grace and mercy. Martha has a long way to go, and her old image of God continues to haunt her from time to time. But she is now able to read her Bible, and she enjoys studying God's Word with other Christians, in a home Bible study group—something she could never have done a few years ago.

During the latency stage of spiritual growth, your child needs to continue internalizing God as a reliable, positive, personal object. Your child also needs to learn more about Christianity, as a foundation for future Christian growth (this is true even if your child has never made a decision to accept Christ as Savior). Continue the same training, by word and by example, that you began in previous stages. You should also provide guidance and direction for your child's new drives and needs, and an environment in which your child can develop an individual relationship with God. Encourage your child to look up to God and depend on him on a daily basis, and suggest ways in which your child can serve others out of Christlike love. Urge your child to keep short accounts with God, to confess sin and to trust God's forgiveness daily. Teach your child to love and forgive others. Create an open environment in which your child feels free to discuss problems and seek spiritual answers from you and from God's Word.

How much spiritual information can a child understand at this stage? Early in this stage, around ages six to eight, children take spiritual concepts literally. For example, though liberal theologians might consider heaven and hell to be metaphors, children at this stage take these concepts for what they really are: spiritual realities. In their literal thinking, children sometimes come up with interesting questions, such as this one posed by a young girl in Sunday school: "What happens to the fire when it rains in hell?"

During ages eight through twelve, as cognitive skills broaden, so does a child's ability to comprehend more difficult spiritual concepts at deeper intellectual and personal levels. For example, children at age twelve can potentially understand supernatural, invisible concepts such as the fact that God is a Spirit, not a human being. At this point, children are capable of relating not only to Jesus, "the Word made flesh," but also to God the Father and God the Holy Spirit.

At this age, a child's experience with prayer may take new forms. Until now, his prayer may consist only of concrete requests such as, "Help my puppy get well," prayed only at bedtime or family devotions, when parents invite him to pray. At ten to twelve years old, a child may actually pray when alone, to cope with feelings of anxiety, fear, guilt, or loneliness. At this stage, the child may be able to cognitively understand and verbalize the essence of his faith to others.

Continue the practical parenting steps for the previous stage, such as those listed below.

Create a pleasant spiritual atmosphere at home. Not a monastery or a legalistic boot camp.

Play with your child. Fun builds relationships and warm memories, and these experiences enhance the child's view of God as a warm, relational being.

Exhibit the fruit of the Spirit. Be an example of Spirit-controlled, Christlike character to your child.

Listen to Christian music. Select music that is geared to the child's age, interests, and tastes. There is a lot of lively, quality Christian music for young people that can enhance your child's spiritual understanding and experience. You don't have to shield a child from all secular music, but some kids, around ages ten or twelve, may become interested in harmful forms of rock music, so exercise parental responsibility in this area.

Maintain a habit of regular devotions. But keep them brief, or they will become torturous and unpleasant for the child. Save long prayers for your private devotions.

Discuss God at mealtimes and throughout the day. Find creative ways to make God a constant companion, a member of the family.

Buy your child good Christian books that are fun and age appropriate.

Take opportunities to relate your child's daily experience to Bible stories and biblical principles.

In addition to these steps, here are additional practical steps you can follow in guiding your child's development toward spiritual security in the latency stage.

Invite your child to accept Jesus Christ as Lord and Savior. This is clearly the number one spiritual task your child needs to achieve—and this is the stage in which most children are spiritually ready and receptive. Remember, not all children develop at the same rate; all spiritual "time clocks" are different. You should not push this decision on your child arbitrarily, but if it is the right timing for your child, then you should explain the gospel to your child and invite him to make that commitment to God. It is possible for many six-year-olds to have enough spiritual awareness and conscience to experience a genuine repentance for their sins and to accept Jesus Christ as Savior. As your child gets older, he will learn more about related abstract concepts. For now, your child only needs to believe. This is one of the most exciting, moving, blessed experiences you can ever share with your child.

Discipline with consistency and love, not anger. Consistent and affirming discipline is crucial. Love should always be offered freely and unconditionally, even in the face of tough discussions, bad behavior, and bad report cards. Children must know where the boundary lines are and which consequences follow which actions. Parents cannot always be one hundred percent fair, but children should know that their parents always *try* to be fair. The most profound biblical teaching on discipline can be summed up in Ephesians 6:4: "Fathers, do not exasperate your children; instead, bring them up in the training and instruction of the Lord." In other words, don't inflict emotional wounds on your children that will make them feel angry and bitter for the rest of their lives. Instead, nurture them, train them, meet their emotional needs. When you do that, you are raising them to have a healthy relationship with their loving heavenly Father.

Inconsistent, erratic punishment tends to create spiritual distrust within the child. Parents who display conditional love, who punish their children out of anger, and who practice discipline that varies according to their internal tension barometer invariably bring harm to their children. Inconsistent discipline causes children to live in fear, never knowing what will set mom or dad off. Those who feel wary around their parents in childhood tend to feel wary around God in adulthood. They expect God to have the same erratic temper as their parents, and they are continually fearful of God's unexpected anger and retaliation.

Continually reassure your child of your love for him, and of the fact that he is lovable and valued. At this stage, children commonly feel inferior, inadequate, incompetent, and unlovable. Since they do not believe in themselves or trust themselves, they often project their feelings of self-hate onto others and onto God, creating a fantasy that God and others also hate them. Children who are allowed or made to feel inferior can, in extreme cases, become seriously antiself, anti-God, and antisocial. Parents who continually communicate love and positive self-worth to their children create an environment that nourishes the child emotionally, spiritually, and socially.

Adolescent Stage: Spiritual Identity vs. Spiritual Confusion

As a parent you have finally reached the stage where the spiritual foundation laying in your child is, for the most part, finished. This does not mean your contributions to your child's spiritual growth are over; rather, the type of contributions you make from this point on will change from a building model to a maintenance model. In a sense, you will be refining and maintaining the foundation of faith which has already been laid. To better prepare yourself for the prementoring role that you will be taking on with your teenager, study the key components of the adolescent stage.

Spiritual Foundation Stone: Searching vertically for meaning and purpose in life, through Christ

Primary Tasks: (1) Comes to the point of salvation (if not achieved in previous stage), (2) accepts self as valued and worthwhile to God, (3) develops hope and faith for the future and for facing unknowns, (4) develops close dependence on God, and (5) controls self constructively through a Holy Spirit-led conscience

During the adolescent stage, teenagers search for individual spiritual identity, spiritual meaning, and purpose in life.

As your teenager embarks on this search, your primary role as a parent is to provide a consistent, godly example and spiritual guidance in his search for meaning. Your goal: to point your adolescent child vertically toward the reality of the presence and power of Christ. Teenagers are tough and skeptical. Whatever you tell your teenager, he will only believe what he can validate by his experience or by your example, past or present. If you have practiced what you have preached, he will tend to honor and heed your counsel. The following are some significant contributions you can make to your teenager's spiritual growth.

Be someone your teenager can trust. It is important that your teenager experience you as a reliable source of help, wisdom, integrity, and affirmation throughout the stages of his emotional and spiritual development, so that he will look to you and to God as a guide in his search for meaning. He will tend to follow your example in searching for his identity, so you should be accessible for help, without forcing decisions on him. As a teenager reaching for independence, he continues to need parental love, acceptance, understanding, support, forgiveness, trust, and freedom (with appropriate controls). As he receives these emotional supports on a consistent basis, he will more easily turn to God (independently of mom and dad) for these needs.

Be a reflection of your heavenly Father. Model God's fatherhood in your life, through your parenthood of your teenage child. Your heavenly Father listens to you, loves and forgives you, is patient, never forsakes you, and never forces you to decide his way but allows you to make your own choices according to your own free will. It is important that you practice this same parenting style with your own teenager as he reaches for adulthood, while encouraging your teen—in word and example—to choose God's will over self-will.

Pass on relationships, not religion. Dangerous and destructive cultural influences surround our teenagers to a much greater degree than when you and I were teens. Children who grow up with an inadequate spiritual foundation have little hope of spiritual security in the pressure-filled, perilous world of the twenty-first century. If we want to raise children who have a strong, sound relationship with God, we must present and model Christianity to them as a *reality* and a *relationship*, not just a *religion*. Only an authentic, rock-hard relationship with the true and living God can withstand the destructive moral and spiritual forces that lie in wait for our children in the near future. Mere religion is doomed to fail.

As the adolescent enters adulthood, he faces a fork in the road of his spiritual life. Arriving at that fork, his choices are quite simple. In fact, most choices are made many years earlier, even in the first six years of life. This diagram shows the two paths that diverge from this crucial fork in the teenager's path.

Secure and Insecure Spiritual Growth Curves
(Young Adulthood through Late Adulthood 21–65+)

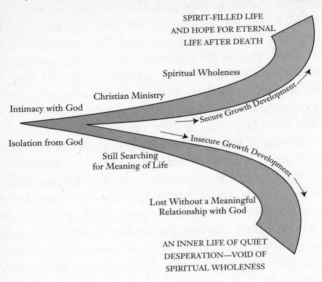

Final Spiritual Growth Curves: Adult Life

WHAT ARE THE TWO CHOICES one has at this spiritual fork in the road? The two spiritual growth life curves in the above diagram illustrate the final three stages of spiritual growth that one will go through, depending on his adult choices and on the pathway that has been set earlier in life. These pathways are significant because they lead the individual into the world of the twenty-first century. They determine whether that individual will be spiritually strong or crumble under the pressure of tomorrow's world. Look at the contrasts between those two paths.

Intimacy with God versus isolation from God. The degree to which one successfully completes the spiritual development tasks from infancy to adolescence largely determines one's ability to achieve intimacy with God. As a developmental task of adulthood, establishing intimacy with God is something that largely takes place in early adulthood, in one's twenties and early thirties. The person who is not able to establish intimacy with God in this stage of life usually tends to always feel isolated from God.

I am not saying that a person with an inadequate developmental foundation can't be saved; I'm saying that many people who are saved never manage to experience a close, satisfying relationship with God. Though accepted by God in reality, they may never feel fully accepted. While forgiven by God in reality, they struggle with feelings of shame and guilt. While they trust Jesus Christ as their Savior, they have trouble relating to God as their Father, and they have difficulty reading his Word.

As Christian parents, we want our children to be saved—but we want more than that. We want them to know a close, satisfying relationship with God. We want them to experience his love and strength daily. We don't want them to feel isolated from God. We don't want our children to think of God as a religious concept, a spiritual token, or a distant energy force. We want them to know God as a Father and as a faithful Friend.

Christian ministry versus a fruitless search for meaning. During middle adulthood—say, mid-thirties to mid-fifties—an individual will generally take one of two spiritual paths. Those adults who have experienced intimacy with God and subsequent spiritual growth are able to share their faith and love of God with others. This sharing takes place through various ministry activities, such as missions work, conducting Bible studies, working with charities, being involved with church, and so forth. Some adults, never having found intimacy with God, find themselves incomplete. They are still searching for meaning—wasting their lives, looking for a sense of purpose in all the wrong places.

Spiritual wholeness versus feeling lost without God. In late adulthood, ages fifty-five plus, we are moving into the final stage of spiritual growth, the stage that completes our spiritual journey and brings us through death, new life, and ultimate sanctification. Even at this last stage, we face a choice between two paths. One road ends in spiritual wholeness. Those who reach this spiritual plateau are able to celebrate the highest degree of the Spirit-filled life, and experience joy and strength in their walk with Christ. They do not fear death but look forward to eternity with God, knowing that they have truly known him and have walked with him.

The other road, sadly, ends void of spiritual wholeness. Those who end up at this spiritual dead end are sentenced to a dismal exile of loneliness and fear, feeling separated from God. In the end, their lives are a wasteland of quiet inner desperation. Death is not seen as a doorway to a new life. It is an end of everything.

As Christian parents, we want our children to experience a close, warm relationship with God, from the time they are born until they stand on the threshold of eternity itself. While it is true that our children are responsible for their own choices through life, we, their parents, have a great deal of influence in shaping their response to life so they will be prepared and encouraged to make the right choices. The key to much that affects a child's future is ultimately in the hands of his parents. The key to your child's image of God is the way you live and the way you represent God to your child. God is counting on you—and your children are counting on you—to give them a hug from God every day. Every hug, every kiss, every affirming, tender word you give your child, is given on behalf of a loving God. When that becomes the way you view your task as a parent, it will transform your view of parenting from a duty to a ministry.

Jesus loves the little children—and he loves them through you and me.

An Awkward Moment

IT WAS THE FIRST time Michael had been by to visit in a couple of months.

"You've really grown, Jen-Jen," he said, lifting Jenea up and holding her in his lap.

"She sure has," Hanna agreed, sitting on the couch across from them.

"Whatcha been up to, kiddo?" Michael asked, giving Jenea a quick tickle and eliciting a laugh.

"I asked Jesus into my heart, Uncle Mike!" Jenea announced happily.

"You did?" said Michael. "Well, that's great, kid, great." He shifted uneasily.

"Did you ever ask Jesus into your heart, Uncle Mike?" asked Jenea.

"Yeah," he answered. "I did once. A long time ago."

"That's good," said Jenea, "because once you do that, Jesus comes to live inside you for ever and ever and ever." She threw her arms around him and gave him a big hug. "I'm glad you have Jesus living in your heart, Uncle Mike, so you can go to heaven with me."

Michael glanced at Hanna. Their eyes met, held for a moment, and then both looked away. "Yeah," Michael said without any sincerity or enthusiasm. "Yeah, I'm glad, too."

NINE

Building Bridges Between Your Child and God

FOR SOME UNEXPLAINED REASON, as he threaded his way along the windy, rain-slick mountain road, Michael thought of Monster.

Monster was an old, gray mongrel dog, as ugly as the day is long—and twice as loyal. Monster had been Michael's best friend from the time Michael was six until he was almost eleven, when Monster died—

Ah, that must be what triggered the memory of his old friend. Michael recalled that his dog had died on a day like this one—rain pouring down in buckets, the sky so dark it seemed like dusk at only three in the afternoon, a dreary, depressing day. The worst day of Michael's life.

Michael had been out in the front yard in his yellow rain slicker, tossing a ball to Monster. Fur soaked and matted, the dog had splashed joyously through puddles in pursuit of that ball, scampering across the road in front of Michael's house, loping through the tall grass of the vacant lot across the road, nosing here and there until he located the ball and chomped down on it. Then, proudly, the dog had run back across the street to Michael, returning the ball in exchange for Michael's affirming "Good dog, Monster" or "Atta boy!"

As he drove, remembering, Michael gripped the steering wheel of his ten-year-old Toyota Celica more tightly, even fiercely. He remembered that it had been a Saturday or a Sunday. It had to be a weekend, because his father was home that day. His dad had come out to yell at him for playing in the rain. As boys will do, Michael had called back, "I'm coming, Dad! Just a minute!" He just wanted to throw the ball for Monster one more time. So he did. And then he threw the ball another time. And another. And another.

And that was when the blue pickup truck had come around the corner too fast. Michael had seen it, and he had called out to Monster to get out of the street. Monster hesitated, dithering back and forth for a moment as the truck came rushing toward him. Maybe if Michael hadn't called out to him, Monster would have kept on going and would have been safely across the street when the truck roared by. But Monster's hesitation in the road kept him rooted to the spot until it was too late.

The driver of the pickup had locked up his brakes in an attempt to stop. The vehicle skidded and fishtailed on the wet pavement, hitting Monster with a sickening smack. Michael watched unbelieving as his dog became a wet raglike thing that flopped and thudded beneath the pickup. The driver ground his gears and sped away, not even looking back.

Michael would never forget what it felt like to run to the street and lift up Monster's head and watch the light and the love go out of those soulful brown eyes. "I'm sorry," he had said over and over to his dead friend as his tears spilled out of his eyes and mingled with the rain on his cheeks. "I'm sorry, Monster! I'm sorry."

Then, looking up, Michael had seen his father striding down the driveway toward him. "What happened, Son?"

Crouching over Monster, the strong, musty smell of the dog's wet fur in his nostrils, Michael had sobbed out, "Monster's dead!" For a moment it seemed as if J. W. were about to walk over to Michael and put his arms around him and comfort him. The man started to take a step forward—then stopped, standing at the edge of the driveway, looking down at his son, arms straight down at his sides.

"This is what happens," J. W. Brown had said, "when you disobey your parents. When you break God's law, there's always a price to pay. If you had come into the house when I told you to, this never would have happened."

Darkness fell quickly as Michael drove on through the rain. He turned on his headlights and tried to think of something else. But he couldn't.

As he drove, Michael could feel the pain of that memory as sharply as if Monster had just died in his arms. He could see the scene in his mind's eye, with just as much clarity and intensity as if it were happening before his own eyes. He could still smell the wet fur and feel the cold rain seeping into him, underneath that yellow slicker. He could still hear the sound of his father's voice, telling him that it was his own fault that Monster was dead. Most of all, he could feel the weight of the guilt his father had piled onto his grief and anguish over the loss of his dog.

Michael's eyes blurred momentarily. He took one hand off the steering wheel to brush the wetness from them, and he tried to clear the painful lump from his throat. He wanted to scream at someone—at God, at his father, at whoever was responsible for the pain he felt inside. The wind that stirred the trees rushing past on either side, and the rain that pounded against his windshield, seemed like God's anger directed against him, opposing him, buffeting him, filling him with a cold misery. Silly idea. Michael didn't even believe in God. How could a nonexistent God be angry with you?

As he brushed the moisture from his eyes, something flashed past beside the road, an orange sign. It went by too fast for him to read it. Ahead, another emergency sign lay fallen in the road where the wind had knocked it down. It lay face up and he tried to read it, even cranking his head around as he drove past, hoping to see it behind him. When he turned back around, he saw that he was coming to a blind curve around a hill. He braked—a little too hard. The car slewed going into the curve, but Michael quickly got it under control.

Coming around the curve, he was suddenly confronted by a confusing scene, all distorted and smeared by the rain and his windshield wipers. Road flares on the ground. A thicket of warning signs. A couple of county trucks parked beside the road, and three or four men standing around, waving him to stop. Now he could read the signs up ahead: one read FLOODING and another read BRIDGE OUT. Beyond the signs was a bridge abutment—and beyond the abutment, where the bridge itself should have been, was darkness and emptiness. Michael hit his brakes, but the car kept going, hydroplaning on the wet road.

Canyons and Rivers to Cross

YOU ARE GOD'S ROAD builder. God has given you the task of paving the way for your child's journey to faith and eternity. The road ahead is not a smooth and level one. There are hills and valleys and even some canyons and rivers in the way. Your child will need more than just a smooth paved surface. He will need bridges to carry him over the canyons and raging rivers of life. He will need spiritual bridges—bridges between himself and God—in order to successfully complete the journey of faith.

Many parents, unfortunately—including all too many *Christian* parents—unwittingly burn the spiritual bridge between their child and God. They may mean well, they may surround their child with religious activity and religious information, but they do not strengthen and support the bridge of *relationship* between their child and God. If that bridge of relationship has been burned in childhood, the child will not be able to cross over it upon becoming an adult in the perilous world of tomorrow.

There are a number of specific bridges that you are called by God to build for the child he has placed in your care. The first bridge, of course, is *you*. You must build the bridge of yourself so that your child can take his first steps toward God. How do you build the bridge of yourself? By being connected to God through daily reliance upon his Word, by obedience to his will, by seeking his guidance through faith, by talking to him and listening to him in prayer. When you remain firmly anchored to God, you cannot help but model God to your child. You cannot help but pass along the nurturing your child needs as you receive that nurturing directly from your heavenly Father. If you do these things, you will be a strong, reliable bridge enabling your child to cross the uneven, rocky places of childhood.

If you choose, however, to disconnect from God's fellowship or just halfheartedly connect with him, you become nothing more than a weak, broken, or burned bridge. Your child's steps toward God can go no closer to him than the bridge of your life will allow. If your child comes to the bridge of your life and finds a sign that reads BRIDGE OUT—DO NOT CROSS he will turn and go another direction.

Here are some of the ways you build a bridge across the canyons and raging rivers of your child's spiritual journey.

- Modeling and teaching unconditional love and acceptance
- Disciplining in love, not in anger
- Guiding toward self-discipline, obedience, and respect for authority
- Training by consistent attitude, instruction, and example
- Pointing away from cultural deceptions and toward reliance upon Christ

Now let's examine some of the canyons and rivers that your child must face along the way—and ways you can help your child bridge those gulfs and continue on toward God.

Bridging the First Gulf: Your Child's Expectations of God

FROM OUR EARLIEST CHILDHOOD experience of faith, we all have expectations of God. Some of those expectations are healthy and realistic, some are unhealthy and unrealistic. Unhealthy expectations rooted in an unrealistic view of God are a deep canyon between a child and God. If the child is not able to bridge that canyon, his faith may not be able to move beyond that deep place in his life.

Nine-year-old Lisa was brokenhearted when her older brother, Brad, lost his battle with leukemia. She had prayed to God ever since her brother was first diagnosed, and she really believed that God would give her brother a miracle of healing. After her brother's death, the disillusioned child went to her grandmother and said, "Grandma, I don't want to pray to God anymore. I'm mad at him, and I don't want to talk to him as long as I live. God doesn't keep his promises, and he doesn't listen to me. If he did, Brad would still be alive."

Is Lisa wrong? She is, after all, only reaching the same conclusions many adults reach in similar circumstances. But certainly God does not fail to keep his promises. Certainly he listens to our prayers, doesn't he? Yes, and he answers our prayers—but not always in the way we expect. If God does not meet our expectations, then the problem is not with God but with our expectations. Lisa's faith has taken a major blow because her expectations of God were unrealistic. Like many other children in today's world—and many adults—she has been taught to believe that God is like Santa Claus or the genie in the bottle, and we can ask any wish of him and he will grant it. Lisa's parents never prepared her for the reality of who God is, and the fact that when God answers prayer, the answer is sometimes no.

It's hard for a child to understand that a loving God can allow her brother—a boy with his entire life ahead of him—to die of leukemia. It's hard for an adult to understand. But that is the reality of God. We build bridges between our children and God when we help them understand that prayer is not a means by which we control what God does but the means by which we communicate—two ways, both talking and listening—with God. In prayer, we don't seek to align God's will with our will; we seek to align our will with his—even when that means sorrow and loss.

In the realm of expectations, there are four kinds of Christians in the world.

Those who have overly high expectations of God. These are dependent, often demanding, personalities. They expect God to do it all for them. They blame God for their own errors, for the sin of the world, for the activity of Satan, for the operation of circumstances. It is good that they want God to be involved in their daily affairs, but it is unhealthy and unrealistic—and actually a bit arrogant—to expect God to operate on their personal timetable, to be at their beck and call.

Is it wrong to have high expectations of God? After all, he created the universe. He made us, in all our complexity. If you can't expect a lot from God, who can you expect it from? Throughout the Bible, God gives us many promises. Basing our expectations of God on his promises is perfectly healthy. Problems arise, however, when our expectations of God exceed his promises—that is, when our expectations become unreasonable. Often we think we have derived our expectations from Scripture, when in fact we have merely interpreted Scripture in such a way that it suits our high expectations.

What unreasonable expectations do we often place on God? We expect God to answer our prayers on our terms, in the time frame of our choosing, in the way that suits our wants. We expect God to perform dramatic miracles to solve our problems and to prop up our sagging faith. We expect God to protect us from all hurt, misfortune, and disappointment. We expect God to rescue us from the consequences of our sin and folly. We expect God to keep us emotionally charged up and exhilarated. If these expectations are not met, many of us become angry or disappointed with God.

Those who have low expectations of God. These personalities expect God to act only during a crisis or when they want or need something. God is not an integral part of their daily lives. These are relatively self-sufficient people who only look to God on special occasions or under special circumstances. To them, God is "911"—a number you call only in emergencies. These are often prideful people who resent God's "interference" in their lives and only want him involved in their lives if they invite him. A certain degree of self-sufficiency can be healthy—if a person can still relate to God, look to him for insight, strength, and wisdom, while taking full responsibility for his or her choices.

Those who have no expectations of God. These are very self-sufficient personalities, frequently addicted to control, having severe problems with their capacity for trust. They are often angry with God for past experiences with him, or childhood experiences with parents. Many were abused, neglected, or seriously disappointed during childhood. They decided long ago never to depend on anyone again—especially someone they cannot see. If they have no expectations of God, they reason, then God will never be able to let them down.

Those who have healthy, realistic expectations of God. Such people have usually been raised with a firm, reliable foundation throughout the stages of their emotional development. They have been taught realistic truths about God: he is a loving Father, he is involved in our lives, he listens to our prayers, *but we do not control him with our prayers.* His ways are not our ways. Ultimately, like Job, we must submit our will to his and recognize that we do not have the right to judge our Creator; it is he who has the right to judge us.

As parents, you can build a bridge of healthy expectations between your children and God, through the three steps below.

Carefully study the promises of God. Know what the Bible says—and what it does not say—about what you can expect from God. Understand that when you pray in the name of Jesus, that doesn't just mean tacking the words "In Jesus' name, Amen" onto the end of your prayers. It means you pray according to the *authority* and the *will* of Jesus, and for the *glorification* of Jesus. If you pray for or expect anything that is outside his authority and will or would not bring glory to him, then the will of Jesus must supersede your will.

Match your expectations of God to the promises of God. If your expectations are too high or too low, adjust them to match the truth of God's promises in Scripture. Invite God to be involved in your life in a dynamic and real way, while acknowledging that he has the right to choose how, when, where, and if he will act in your life. Acknowledge that he is God, not you, and accept his Word as the final word on all your circumstances.

Communicate your healthy expectations to your children. Teach them verbally, in various life situations. "Yes," you might say, "I have been praying that I would get this promotion, but God did not see fit to allow it to happen right now." Or, "Yes, we prayed that we would have a safe trip, but there was a drunk driver on the road, and we had an accident, and Daddy's in the hospital. But God can use even a situation like this one. Maybe there is someone in the hospital that Daddy can tell about Jesus. Let's pray that God will bring something very good out of this bad situation." Let your child hear your humility and obedience coming through in your prayers. Just as Jesus humbly, obediently prayed in Gethsemane, surround your prayers with an attitude of "Not my will but yours be done."

You and your children can realistically expect God to

- Love unconditionally
- Forgive and show mercy

- Support and encourage you through the Holy Spirit
- Listen to your prayers
- Be patient with you
- Discipline you in love (behavior produces consequences)
- Remain unchangeable and reliable
- Never forsake you or reject you
- Provide the things you truly need for a life of contentment and peace
- Answer your prayers on his timetable and on his terms
- Never lie to you or break a promise

If God will do all these things for you, what can you and your child realistically expect God *not* to do? He will not give you everything you want or ask for just because you ask in his name. He will not fix you breakfast in bed. He will not put a Lincoln Town Car in your driveway. He will not take away all your problems. He will not cut your taxes. He will not get you a part in a Hollywood movie, or a starting position on the Orlando Magic basketball team. He will not be manipulated (don't give a hundred dollars to a televangelist and expect God to send you a check for a hundred thousand dollars by return mail). He will not do anything for you that you can (and should) do for yourself.

God will not force you to do anything against your will. He will encourage, guide, influence, and convict you through the Holy Spirit, but he will not bend or break your will. He will not make your choices for you, nor will he accept responsibility for your choices.

God will not change the past. He will not take away your painful memories. He will help you heal the pain of the past, and he will help you take the sting out of your memories and learn from your memories. But God will not alter time and space in order to make your life more comfy.

God will not remove all temptation, trials, sin, harm, risk, disaster, or negative consequences from your life. He has not promised to take you *out* of the world and its troubles; he has promised to take you *through* it.

God will not trick you or play games with you. He will not put obstacles in your way or hurt you. When life tricks you or obstructs you or hurts you, that is not God—that is the world and Satan and circumstances. God has not promised to protect you against such things. He has promised to use these events in your life to make you more like Jesus Christ, to build your character, and to teach you about his love and support in times of trial and testing.

God will not make life fair. Ever since sin came into the world, life has been horribly unfair. It was not fair that Jesus, who was completely innocent, had to die for our sins. But that is the way God works. He dispenses something in our lives that is even greater than fairness. He dispenses grace, mercy, and love. Don't expect God to be fair. Instead, expect him to love you and show grace to you even when life is horribly unjust.

These are healthy expectations of God. You build a bridge between your children and God by teaching them to have these kinds of healthy expectations of their heavenly Father. It is a bridge that will take them one step further along their journey of faith.

Bridging the Second Gulf: Your Child and the Problem of Sin

SIN FORMS A MAJOR gulf between your child and God, producing feelings of shame, guilt, and unworthiness. Teaching children how to deal with sin and receive forgiveness builds a bridge that leads to greater emotional and spiritual security and a stronger relationship between your child and God.

Many children from religious homes, unfortunately, are saturated with an unhealthy view of sin that creates a lifelong barrier between themselves and God. Todd was one of these people. All his life, as far back as he could remember, he had heard that "God hates sinners." Coming from an extremely legalistic home and church environment, he heard this message again and again as he was growing up. He looked around at his parents and at the people in his church, and all he saw was perfect Christians. He never heard his dad admit to committing any sin or making any mistakes.

Then Todd looked at his own life. He continually found himself making mistakes, committing sins, telling a lie here, fighting with his sister there, harboring an angry thought toward his father, sneaking money from his mother's purse to buy some baseball cards. Whenever he did such things, he felt not only guilty but scared. He was convinced that God hated him, and he was afraid to go to God and confess his sin, knowing that God could never forgive a sinner. He tried not to sin. He wanted to live a perfect life, but he couldn't, no matter how hard he tried. He wondered what was wrong with him that he couldn't be perfect like his parents and the perfect, sinless Christians in his church.

Finally, reaching adolescence, Todd concluded that he would always be hated by God—and that he would always hate God in return. After all, God must have made him defective, since he was unable to keep from sinning like other Christians. It must be God's fault that he couldn't be perfect. Yet he could never quite bring himself to totally reject God, because the fear of hell had been drilled into him since childhood.

When Todd came to me for counseling, he was thirty years old—and he had not been to church for eleven years. During his first session, Todd said, "Dr. Stephens, the reason I don't go to church is that I don't want to be a hypocrite. Since I know in my heart I'm not completely repentant about certain sins, and since I know God can see my heart, I figure what's the use in playing games with God and church? God wouldn't forgive me anyway, and I can't be any worse off with God by not faking my unwillingness to turn over complete control of my life to him."

Todd's story is a familiar one in my counseling experience. He had never been taught such concepts as forgiveness, repentance, or sanctification. He viewed the Christian life as an all-or-nothing proposition: you are either sinless and perfect, or you are damned and hated by God. Because all the Christians around him—including his parents—maintained a false front of spiritual perfection and because none of them ever admitted to any faults or sins, Todd thought he was the only sinner in a church filled with perfect saints. He was astonished to discover, during our counseling sessions, that *everyone* sins. He was even more astonished to find verse after verse in the Bible showing that God expects Christians to confess their sins, to repent of their sins, and to be forgiven of their sins; all his life, he thought the Bible taught that to be a genuine Christian, a person must *never* sin. That just isn't so.

Today Todd is growing spiritually, attending church, and reading his Bible. Day by day he is flushing the old toxic beliefs of legalism out of his system and learning to live by God's grace. He is amazed to find that by the grace of God, he is able to have much more power over sin and temptation than he ever had under legalism and the fear of God's hatred.

A child who moves into the twenty-first century with an unhealthy view of sin risks turning away from God altogether (as Todd tried to do for many years) or joining a cult or false religious movement that preaches acceptance without rules and laws. To secure your child's spirituality in the perilous world of tomorrow, build a bridge of God's grace over the gulf of sin.

Teach your child that while God hates sin, he loves the sinner. Teach him that while sin affects our relationship with God, it does not cause God to abandon us or hate us. Show your child by example how God, our heavenly Father, loves us, his children, even when we sin. When your child sins, express your sorrow over his sin, but also the fact that you love him and want to restore him and forgive him—and tell him that God's love and forgiveness is even greater than yours. Teach and demonstrate the way of confession that leads to grace and forgiveness. Though "all have sinned," as the Bible tells us, God is always ready to forgive our sins and cleanse us from guilt, shame, and unrighteousness.

Bridging the Third Gulf: Your Child's Emotions

EMOTIONS ARE ALWAYS REAL—BUT emotions are not always true. Sometimes our feelings lie.

We often base our beliefs about God on our feelings rather than on the objective truth of God's Word. Feelings, however, do not know what is real or not real. Feelings do not distinguish between what is true and what is not true. While our rational mind is capable of comprehending objective reality, our emotions often send us false messages: "I *feel* ashamed and unworthy; God must hate me." "I don't *feel* saved; maybe I didn't pray the right words, or maybe I don't believe the right doctrines." "I confessed my sin and asked God to forgive me, but I still *feel* guilty, so I guess God is still angry with me." These feelings are all real—in that we really do feel them—but they are not true. They do not reflect the way God actually views us. They do not reflect the objective, rational truth of the Bible.

We have all experienced this contradiction between our feelings and our rational mind. Watch a scary movie, and your rational mind will say, "It's only a movie." At the same moment, your feelings cause your heart to pound with fear. Your feelings do not know that it is only a movie.

In the same way, our rational mind may read the Bible and say, "God is good; God is love," while our feelings—which may have been damaged by painful circumstances, abuse, or shame in childhood—may say, "I am afraid of God; God is angry with me." People who feel insecure, because of failure to develop emotional security in childhood, often doubt their salvation. They are unable to internalize the continuing presence and love of God. They ask Jesus into their hearts again and again and again—yet they continue to experience God as an object of fear, anxiety, false guilt, and confusion.

Some of the emotions that create a gulf between a child and God are listed below.

Fear. According to Scripture, the opposite of love is fear. "There is no fear in love," says 1 John 4:18. "But perfect love drives out fear, because fear has to do with punishment. The one who fears is not made perfect in love." If we demonstrate love to our children and exemplify God's love to them, we will help them to be made complete in love—and that love will drive out their fears, especially an unhealthy fear of God's anger or punishment.

Shame. Toxic shame originates in early childhood as it is passed down to us from shame-based adults and reinforced by shame-filled experiences in life. Shame results when we internalize the anger or disappointment of others, causing us to believe there is something wrong with us. It is also the poisonous emotional residue of abuse and legalism. Once shame has us in its grip, we go through life filtering all experiences through our sense of inadequacy and shame. We ignore events that would make us feel worthwhile, and focus instead on events that make us seem worthless and shameful. We feel that God can never accept us or forgive us, even though the Scriptures tell us,

> If we confess our sins, he is faithful and just and will forgive us our sins and purify us from all unrighteousness.
>
> 1 John 1:9

> Your sins have been forgiven on account of his name.
>
> 1 John 2:12

> In him we have redemption through his blood, the forgiveness of sins, in accordance with the riches of God's grace that he lavished on us with all wisdom and understanding.
>
> Ephesians 1:7–8

The message we give to our children, over and over again, must be the message of God's rich, lavish grace—grace that is greater than any sin or shame, grace that invests each of us with enormous worth and value.

Anger. There is nothing sinful about the emotion of anger per se. Anger is a survival mechanism, and we use it to take emotional pain and expel it outward from ourselves. But if we allow anger to build up in us, it turns into bitterness, resentment, malice, grudges, hatred, self-hatred, and depression. Anger must be managed daily, situation by situation, or it builds up and becomes a destructive force within our soul, blocking our relationship with God and with other people. As parents, we need to learn how to manage and express our anger appropriately, not explosively or aggressively. Then we need to teach our children how to manage their anger and express it in a healthy way.

Guilt. Authentic guilt—the response of a conscience to actual sin—is a healthy emotion if we respond to it by repenting (changing our behavior and attitude, and turning back to God) and receiving God's forgiveness. Guilt that is not resolved through repentance and forgiveness festers and becomes poisonous. It destroys our joy and our sense of being loved by God. It blocks our fellowship with God. False guilt—a generalized sense of being dirty, evil, unacceptable, or unforgiven by God, even though there is no specific sin to be repented of—is common among people who have been raised in a legalistic or shame-based home environment. God does not want his children to be defeated and burdened by guilt of any kind, so he has made it possible for us to be fully and freely forgiven. If we still feel guilty despite the fact that we have confessed and repented of our sin and asked God to forgive us, then there are probably emotional issues that need to be dealt with in our lives. If we take the steps to remove guilt from our lives (for example, by going into therapy with a Christian counselor and dealing with the underlying reasons for our guilt feelings), then we can break the cycle and avoid passing on the emotion of guilt to our children.

Worry and Anxiety. Worry is a fear response to imagined circumstances that may or may not happen in the future. Anxiety is a generalized fear of unknown dangers or losses. These are common emotions, but they run counter to the life of faith. If we are worried or anxious, then we are not trusting God for all our circumstances. If we are trusting God, then we are not worried or anxious. Worry-anxiety and trust-faith are mutually exclusive conditions. The worried mind says, "God can't handle this situation. I have to control it. God is going to let something terrible happen to me." Our goal as parents is to learn to trust God for all our circumstances, to model that trust to our children, and to teach them that God is real, he is in control, and he can be trusted.

The best way to teach children how to manage their emotions is by consistently modeling emotional maturity and godliness. Teach your child to accept his feelings, by accepting him when he is undergoing negative emotions. In times of highly charged emotion in the family, turn to God in prayer and let each family member honestly express his or her emotions to God. You help to build a bridge between your child and God when you enable him to deal with his feelings in a healthy way.

Michael at the Bridge: The Story Continues

SOMETHING TOLD MICHAEL TO ease off the brake and steer gently to the right. As he did so, Michael felt the wheels of the car make a tentative grab at the slick surface of the road. The car lurched to the right, heading for the concrete abutment. Everything seemed to happen in slow motion. Michael thought, *Better to hit concrete than to go flying off into the river.*

Something told him to lean down across the seat. He obeyed without thinking. When the car hit the abutment, the steering wheel drove straight into the place where his chest and face had been a split instant before. There was a grinding of steel and a shower of glass. Michael could sense the car collapsing like an accordion around him. He felt strange, almost weightless, as the Toyota went up on its nose, twisted crazily, then fell onto its roof. He heard the sound of crumpling sheet metal, the groan of the frame, a hubcap popping loose and bouncing across the asphalt.

Then for a few moments all he could hear was the rain tapping against the underside of the upended car. Michael sensed that the car had come to rest on a slope, possibly the riverbank itself. The dashboard was pressed up against his face, and his right arm was wedged between the seat and his body. His left arm was pinned behind his back, the seat belt was cutting into his middle, and his knees were jammed underneath the steering column. He expected to feel pain, incredible pain, but for now all he felt was a dull, cold sensation in his left knee.

Just then he heard the shouts from the men along the road. For the first time in years, Michael began to pray.

Bridging the Fourth Gulf: The Valleys of Life

ALL FAMILIES AND INDIVIDUALS travel over hills and through deep valleys at different times in life. The valleys of life can either draw a child closer to God—or drive that child away from God. It often depends on the parents' attitudes and the spiritual preparation of that child in the home.

Brenda was a patient of mine, in her thirties, whose five-year-old daughter had been killed by a drunk driver. She struggled through her grief and managed to go on with her life with her faith intact. A few years passed, however, and then her husband was also killed in a car accident. When I heard this, I made numerous attempts to call Brenda and finally reached her (she had moved out of state a few years earlier).

Not surprisingly, I found Brenda to be very changed, very shaken, and very deeply wounded by her incredible losses. Her relationship with God had been noticeably clouded. "Dr. Stephens," she said, "what did I do? Why is God angry with me? Why has he taken away everyone I love?" Brenda had gone deep into one of life's valleys, and the experience had made her wonder if there was some unknown sin in her life that had caused an angry God to judge her.

Frank, a tough-minded truck driver, told me he had been angry with God ever since his father died of a heart attack when he was nine years old. "I've had a grudge against God," he said, "ever since I stood at that graveside and watched my father being lowered into the ground in a box. Whenever I hear someone talk about the love of God, I think, *Man, what a pack of lies!*" Frank came to the Minirth Clinic shortly after his mom was diagnosed with a terminal illness. "God is the Terminator, Dr. Stephens," he told me. "God is the Hangman. Everyone I love God takes away. He's not fair. He's not loving. He's a cosmic sadist. He took my sister in a head-on collision three years ago, and now my mom has terminal cancer."

I hear Brenda's questions about God, and Frank's accusations against God, on a daily basis at the clinic. I can't blame either of them for the way they feel. Many people encountering one of life's deep valleys wonder why God is hurting them. In fact, however, God doesn't want to hurt us; he wants nothing more than to heal us. Most of the trials we experience in life are the result of evil in the world—either the evil of satanic activity or the evil stirred up by human free will. Our God is not sadistic. He is loving. And our children desperately need to know what God is really like as they prepare to move into the troubled world of the twenty-first century. If Christians ascribe every negative event in their lives to God, then: (1) they are blaming God and claiming to know his mind, when in reality his ways are far beyond our ways and our understanding; and (2) in doing so, they will likely end up feeling angry and resentful toward God.

All of us make assessments about who God is, based on the experiences we go through and the events we witness. It is only natural that we attribute the cause of many of these experiences and events to God. If a family member dies, we wonder, "Why did God take my loved one?" When a typhoon kills thousands in Bangladesh, or a plane crash kills hundreds on a mountainside, we wonder, "How could God cause or allow that to happen?" If we suffer year after year with a soul-grinding chronic illness or with a severe financial problem that never seems to get better, we want to know, "How can God put me through this unending trial? Can't he see I've suffered enough?"

What should we attribute to God, according to the Bible? All that is good in our lives, from our most exhilarating joys to the simplest pleasures of a warm, sunny day. Most of us, however, tend to attribute both positive and negative experiences to God, even though the Bible firmly declares that God loves us and that everything he does in our lives is good. There are psychological as well as spiritual reasons why we attribute both good and bad experiences to God. By making God the one to praise in the good times and blame in the bad times, we feel that we can somehow maintain a measure of control over our world. Believing that there is a reason for everything that happens in the world—even if it is a reason known only to God—enhances our sense of security.

Either because of a desire to blame God for the painful experiences of our lives or because of an inadequate understanding of Scripture, some of us interpret the Bible so that it seems to make God the author of evil events. For example, some people read 1 Peter 1:6–7, which encourages Christians to view trials as a test of the genuineness of their faith, and then they say, "It says right here that God is testing me!" These people miss the point of the passage. Peter is not telling us that God deliberately sends trials to us. He is saying that trials—which are simply an inevitable part of life for Christians and non-Christians alike—can be *used* by God as tests to demonstrate the quality of our faith. God doesn't inflict testing on us, but since testing is inevitable in life, he doesn't want its lessons to be wasted. The purpose of testing is not to prove our faith to God—he knows the level of our faith better than we know it ourselves. He uses these experiences in our lives to demonstrate the durability of our faith *to ourselves*. Trials and testing enable us to discover what we are made of and what we can accomplish and endure with the strength and encouragement of God.

The Bible does not tell us that God inflicts pain and suffering on his people. But when suffering comes, God is able to transform that suffering into something good. That is precisely the point of a key passage on the subject of attributing experiences to God: "And we know that in all things God works for the good of those who love him, who have been called according to his purpose. For those God foreknew he also predestined to be conformed to the likeness of his Son, that he might be the firstborn among many brothers" (Rom. 8:28–29). In other words, God has a purpose for all things that happen to us, and his ultimate purpose for us is that we be "conformed to the likeness" of Christ—that is, that our character and nature be gradually molded and shaped to resemble the character of Jesus himself.

A paradox is at work in the world. God is sovereign and in ultimate control. However, many things that happen in the world do not happen according to his will. The key to this paradox is human free will. He will not exercise his control to negate our free moral choices or to protect us from the painful valleys of life. We do not understand how God can be in control and still allow bad things to happen to us. But we trust God, knowing that someday we will understand, because his ways are different from our ways, and his ways are just and righteous.

These are the lessons Frank is learning day by day in the aftermath of the valleys he has encountered. Today he is at a different place than he was soon after the tragic death of his sister. During his counseling visits, we focused a lot of attention on his feelings about his losses, and the fact that he attributed these losses to God. Though he continues to struggle with mixed feelings toward God, Frank is experiencing a growing realization that God is not his enemy, that there are destructive forces in the world that God mysteriously allows but does not cause, and that he will only find a secure and satisfied life when he is able to stop blaming God for the painful valleys in his life.

You have certainly been through valleys of your own, and you may even be in one right now. But don't forget that there are little souls going through that valley with you. They don't have the understanding or strength you have, and they are watching you to see how you handle the hard places in life. You are their model of faith. What are they learning from you about the reality of God's strength and faithfulness in the deep places, the low places, the valleys of life?

You build a bridge between your child and God by providing a positive example of how to walk through valleys in mature Christian faith. Some practical ways to turn valleys into bridges for your child's spiritual journey are shown below.

- Be honest about your feelings and your sadness in difficult times (don't teach your children to repress their emotions), but do so without blaming God for your problems. If you have anger toward God, take those feelings to a pastor or counselor and work through them—don't air them in front of your children.

- When going through valleys, maintain spiritual disciplines such as church attendance, Bible reading, and prayer. Be sure to pray with your children so they see that your connection to God remains strong.

- Teach your child that it is okay to share questions with God about the valley you are in. When you pray with your children, it's okay to say, "God, we don't understand why this is happening. Please give us wisdom to trust you more." Avoid saying, "God, why are you doing this to us? What did we ever do to make you mad at us?"

- Assure your child that valleys in life do not necessarily mean that people are bad or that God is punishing them.

- In your family devotions, examine Bible stories in which God has been present and has carried people through the valleys of life.

- Stay tuned in to your child's feelings. Do not assume that your child is handling the valley as well as you are. Keep the lines of communication between you and your child clear and open.

The Church as a Bridge to God

I HAVE BEEN A Christian counselor for ten years, and the single greatest reason I hear from people who have abandoned church attendance is the negative religious training that was forced upon them in their early life. Our faith in God is founded in large part on what we are taught as children in church, Sunday school, Christian school, and at home. Our early instruction can have both positive and negative effects on our relationship with God.

Of all the people I have counseled, the most tragic cases have tended to be those who were exposed to rigid legalism in their early religious life. They tend to see God as an unmerciful judge and a stern taskmaster. If they do not attain perfection according to the strict demands of their legalistic beliefs—and no one can—they expect the blast of God's hot wrath and judgment. They are unable to experience the full range of God's relational personality—his mercy, love, compassion, and empathy—and they live in a spiritual and emotional prison of bondage, fear, and guilt. All this is the result of an unhealthy church environment.

A healthy church, on the other hand, can be one of the most powerful, positive influences on the emotional and spiritual development of your child. What does a healthy church look like? It is a church that

- preaches the gospel of salvation
- accepts the Bible as God's Word, without error yet subject to interpretation
- promotes individual freedom and thought, and allows people to take varying points of view on secondary points of doctrine without being criticized or condemned
- practices genuine love, acceptance, and forgiveness
- builds bridges, not barriers, between people; practices inclusivity rather than exclusivity
- offers laypeople and young people opportunities to discover and use their spiritual gifts in ministry (for example, junior high and high school students are involved in vacation Bible school, ministry trips to help inner-city poor,

and so forth; these experiences help build Christian relationships and solidify a young person's faith experience)
- preaches a positive message about human sexuality—that sex is a gift of God to be used appropriately within marriage, that sex is not merely for procreation but to create emotional and spiritual bonding of husband and wife, as well as mutual pleasure and satisfaction
- teaches grace, not legalism
- provides an effective means of helping people move from guilt to forgiveness
- promotes the belief that self-acceptance is based on God's acceptance
- demonstrates concern for the deeper emotional and mental health of people who struggle with sin, rather than simply condemning sinners
- is known for a spirit of joy and for its rich fellowship experience, not for fear and rigid authority
- offers opportunities for church members to get to know each other, care for each other, pray for each other, and share each other's burdens (small-group Bible studies, support groups, recovery groups, "house churches," and so forth)
- focuses more on wholeness and building well-balanced people than on rules, duties, and controls; seeks to add wings, not weights, to the emotional and spiritual growth of adults and children

A church that teaches the mercy, grace, forgiveness, and love of God is a church that exemplifies the character of God. It provides warm, accepting fellowship for the entire family. A church that gives your child opportunities to discover and use his spiritual gifts can be a firm, supportive bridge on your child's spiritual journey.

The *Real* Miracle

"I CAN'T BELIEVE YOU were only in the hospital one day," said Hanna, eyeing her brother in amazement. They sat at the kitchen table of her home. Michael's face and arms were marked here and there by scratches and abrasions, but miraculously, the only injury he had suffered was a deep cut to his left knee—fortunately, no muscles or ligaments were damaged. After his knee was stitched up, he was released. That was two days ago.

"It took them three hours to cut me out of that car," said Michael. "It was a good thing my leg was pinned, so I didn't bleed to death. I was conscious the whole time. I had a lot of time to think. And I had a lot to think about. I could have gone right into the river, but something told me how to brake and steer so I would hit the bridge abutment instead. I could have been crushed by the steering wheel, but something told me to duck down at just the right moment to save my life. The rescue workers told me there was no way I should have lived through that accident. They called it a miracle. But some of my agnostic friends say it was pure survival instinct."

"I think God's speaking to you, Michael," said Hanna. "I just pray you'll listen for his voice."

"I'm trying, Hanna," said Michael. "If God is really there, if he's really speaking to me, then I want to hear what he has to say. I want to hear him loud and clear. And maybe I'm beginning to—but not because of the accident."

"What do you mean?"

"Dad came over to the apartment for a talk yesterday. And he was crying. In all the years I've known him, I don't think I've ever seen him cry before. I don't think I ever saw him express real emotion before. I mean, that *really* shook me up. He sat down and told me it scared him that I almost died without hearing how sorry he was for the things he did when I was growing up. Like the time he punished me by locking me out of the house all night."

"I remember that," said Hanna with a shudder.

"And the time he berated me for asking how Jesus turned water into wine. And all the times he threatened me with God's wrath and hellfire and all that. And the way he treated me when Monster died."

"Your dog?"

"Yeah."

"Mike, did you bring up all these things and ask him to apologize?"

"No way! He brought it up himself. I just sat there stunned and speechless while he reeled off all these things he had done to me when I was a kid. I never knew he was sorry about that stuff."

"In his own way," said Hanna, "Dad tried to be a good father to us. He wanted to raise us to know God, but he just didn't know how to go about it. But he's changed, Michael."

"You're telling *me* he's changed? Listen, Sis. Let me tell you what he said about when Monster died—something I never knew before. He said that when he saw me there in the road, holding my dead dog in my arms with all that rain coming down, he said he wanted to run to me, pick me up, and hold me. But he couldn't."

"Why not?" asked Hanna.

"That's what I asked him," said Michael. "And he said, 'Because I thought you needed to learn a lesson. I *wanted* to hug you, I really did—but I scolded you instead. That's the way my dad brought me up, and that's the way I tried to bring you and Hanna up. I've only recently learned that sometimes kids need mercy more than they need to learn a lesson. You don't raise a child by pounding lessons into a child's head. You raise a child with love. It's taken me the better part of a lifetime to see how wrong I was.'"

Hanna's mouth dropped open. "*Daddy* said that? *Our* dad—J. W. Brown himself—said that? He's changed even more than I thought!"

"Yeah," Michael nodded in amazement. "And after he said that, he asked me to forgive him. Sis, I don't remember Dad *ever* asking me to forgive him when I was a kid."

"And what did you say, Michael?"

"What could I say? I forgave him—and I asked him to forgive me for the hurt I had caused him. We ..." He hesitated. Hanna could see it was hard for him to continue. "We ... well, we both cried. And then he hugged me. Sis, that was the first time he's hugged me since I was five or six years old!"

Hanna brushed tears from her own eyes.

"You know," Michael continued, his voice quavering, "I can't say for sure if it was a miracle that saved my life during the crash at the bridge. Maybe it was miraculous, maybe just luck. But I *know* a miracle has happened in my life. To me, the *real* miracle is the change in Dad. If God is speaking to me right now, he's speaking to me through the miracle that happened between Dad and me last night."

———

FOR YEARS, THE BRIDGE of understanding between J. W. Brown and his son, Michael, had been washed away by neglect and bitterness. But when Michael nearly lost his life at a washed-out bridge on a storm-drenched mountain road, he and his father got a second chance to rebuild the bridge of love between them. Could the bridge of relationship between Michael and God ever be restored? Only time would tell ...

TEN

Measuring Your Family's Spiritual Security

THIS CHAPTER CONSISTS OF a series of assessments designed to help you understand where your child is spiritually—and where your child is headed. As we have discussed, there are specific stages of spiritual growth, and specific needs that correspond to each of those stages. By determining whether these spiritual needs have been met and whether specific developmental tasks have been achieved at each stage, we can gain a clearer sense of how the child is progressing toward spiritual and emotional maturity.

The first checklist is divided into five categories, each representing a different spiritual development stage. Answer the questions by placing a check mark in front of each statement that describes your child. Evaluate your child at the stage appropriate to his age. (You may also check statements for earlier stages, to gain a sense of how well your child has progressed from birth to the present.)

Assessing Your Child's Current Spiritual Security

MY CHILD HAS DEMONSTRATED that he
Infancy Stage (Birth to Fifteen Months)

___feels safe and secure in my presence
___feels safe and secure in my absence
___responds positively to cuddling, cooing, and stroking

Toddler Stage (Fifteen Months to Three Years)

___feels loved and accepted in my presence
___feels loved and accepted after being left alone

___feels loved and accepted after being told no
___can freely give love verbally and physically
___has started the process of separation-individuation
___is more at peace than angry
___has an acceptable attitude toward authority

Preschool (Three to Six Years)

___believes in the concept of God
___believes God is love
___believes God is good
___believes God is personal
___has the beginnings of a healthy respect and reverence for God
___believes in and trusts God's unconditional love and acceptance
___resolves guilt easily by trusting God to forgive
___is forming his own inner conscience
___has a natural interest in learning about spiritual concepts
___seems to have at least a moderately positive attitude (or not a negative attitude) toward prayer and Bible time
___has a generally positive attitude toward church (setting aside normal preschool frustrations and a short attention span)
___can practice basic obedience

Latency (Approximately Six to Twelve Years)

___has a continued interest in learning spiritual truths
___has accepted Christ or has brought up the need
___is taking the initiative to form his own relationship with God
___has a growing confidence in God's ability to be merciful and forgive
___maintains a positive attitude toward God, his authority, and his claim on our lives
___experiences security in his faith, even during difficult times

___is beginning to show evidence of the fruit of the Spirit in daily life, as listed for us in Galatians 5:22–23: "The fruit of the Spirit is love, joy, peace, patience, kindness, goodness, faithfulness, gentleness and self-control."

Adolescence (Approximately Thirteen to Twenty-one Years)

___has accepted Christ or has brought up the need (if this has not been accomplished in the latency stage)

___is interested in fellowship with other Christian young people

___believes he is worthwhile to God

___feels that God is close and available

___trusts God's grace and forgiveness

___depends on God's promises for support, inner control, and guidance

___looks to God—not self, pleasure, or materialism—for purpose and meaning in life

___is able to choose self-restraint and obedience to God and his authority

___is able to make good decisions, seeking God's will (through the Holy Spirit) over self-will (the flesh)

___begins to comprehend more complex spiritual concepts such as the Holy Spirit and the Trinity

___is able to openly initiate the confession of sin

___begins to act on the truths of the Bible

___demonstrates an interest in the Christian life that supersedes an interest in cultural deceptions such as materialism and secularism

___is self-motivated to worship God in a church setting

___independently seeks a prayer life and devotional life outside the church worship experience

___demonstrates the fruit of the Spirit in a meaningful and daily-increasing way

___can internalize Scripture texts of wisdom and assurance, finding them useful and personally meaningful

___can easily internalize (feel) God's love, finding his love to be real, personal, and meaningful

___can love with both friendship love and Christlike,
      unconditional love

___demonstrates a willingness and ability to forgive others

___rarely doubts his salvation

___can relate to God on a personal level

Evaluating This Assessment

Every one of the items on the checklist represents a developmental task that the child should complete within his given stage of development. Our goal is to be able to honestly check all of the items at each developmental stage. Any item not checked is, in essence, a crack in that child's spiritual and developmental foundation. The earlier the stage, the more crucial each step is to later development. Because so much of an individual's personality is formed by age six, it is crucial that a healthy foundation be built during the first three stages, birth to six years. These are the years when our spiritual foundation is poured like wet cement within the formative, shaping boundaries of our emotions, relationships, and experiences. If those formative boundaries are healthy and secure, then our spiritual wet cement will harden into a firm, sound, solid foundation. If not, our foundation will develop cracks, crumbling, and stress fractures.

A firm foundation in childhood makes it possible for later adolescent and adult faith to be experienced in a personal, powerful, and meaningful way. A weak foundation reduces adolescent and adult faith in God to a series of token rituals that will either be slavishly endured or rejected later in life. In the person with a weak foundation, faith is not built on love and trust but on fear and neurotic guilt. Such a token faith cannot stand the pressures of the new world order of the next century. Those with only a token faith will be easily preyed upon by the vultures of Middle Eastern meditation as a substitute form of spirituality. Those whose faith consists only of token rituals rather than an authentic, living relationship with God will reach a point of realizing that they have not found meaning and fulfillment in their faith— and they will compensate by seeking to fill that void through some other source, such as false religion or false values or the pursuit of things (money, pleasure, power) that cannot ultimately satisfy.

If you find that your child has not completed the spiritual growth tasks of the years from birth to six, it does not mean that you have failed as a parent or that your child is destined to be spiritually handicapped. You can begin now to repair the damaged foundation of your child's personality in two ways.

1. Accept God's mercy and forgiveness for any shortcomings or failures in your past parenting.
2. Commit (perhaps with the help of a therapist or a parents' support group) to repairing the cracks in your child's personality and doing everything possible to give your child a firm spiritual foundation for his future years. Avoid draining your parental energy off into unproductive directions, such as self-hate or self-pity. Instead, make constructive changes in your parenting style so that the remaining stages of your child's spiritual growth will be healthy ones and so that your child can experience healing in areas where brokenness and cracks exist today. Instead of focusing on what went wrong in your child's life, focus on how to make it right.

You'll notice that the developmental tasks listed in the first three stages are fewer in number and more basic than the tasks listed in latency and adolescence. Ideally, a child should achieve all of the tasks for each of the first three stages in order to progress to the next stage. In latency and adolescence, however, the developmental tasks become more complex. Spiritual growth beyond the preschool years is characterized by strong variation among those who are trying to complete the various developmental tasks. Children naturally grow at different rates, depending on a number of variables, including family, culture, personality, temperament, religious training, and so forth. Some spiritual seeds planted in childhood may not bloom until early adulthood.

So you should be concerned with the results of this assessment only to the degree that your child fails in task completion. But where does one draw the line on deciding if a child is spiritually handicapped? Clearly, spirituality is not something we can gauge with scientific precision. However, it is fair to say that a child should have achieved roughly half the tasks for his stage by the time he is midway through that stage.

If this checklist identifies cause for concern about the spiritual development of your child, take time to observe the life of your child. Keep a journal of your child's experiences and responses to different situations. Look for evidence that your child is either accomplishing or failing to accomplish these developmental tasks. Consider the history of your child; you know your child better than anyone else, so think back to previous stages and ask yourself, "Is there a weak point in my child's earlier spiritual foundation?"

For example, if your ten-year-old continually fails to show evidence of a positive attitude toward authority, go back to the toddler section of the above checklist and ask yourself, "As a toddler, did my child feel loved and accepted after being told no?" If the answer is yes, then move to another question. If the answer is no, then you have just discovered one of the weak points in your child's earlier spiritual foundation. At this point, you can begin repairing that crack by making a special effort to demonstrate unconditional acceptance to your child, even in times of discipline. Make a concerted effort to discipline in love, not in anger. If you must impose a punishment—a "time-out" or the loss of a privilege—also give your child a hug to let him know that your discipline is an act of love, not an act of anger or hate. By demonstrating your own unconditional love and acceptance as a parent, you will be modeling God's unconditional love and acceptance—and you will help to repair your child's sense of spiritual insecurity. Your choice to actively, aggressively repair the early flaws in your child's spiritual and emotional foundation can help to strengthen his spiritual security into adolescence and adulthood.

Continue this process until you have identified each uncompleted developmental task and formed a plan for each of the spiritual "repairs" you must make. Share your commitment with another trusted person (a pastor, counselor, close friend, or someone in a parents' support group or home Bible study) so that person can pray for you and hold you accountable, checking in with you from time to time about your progress.

Where Are *You* Spiritually?

TILL NOW, WE HAVE focused on your child's spiritual growth needs and current condition. Now let's examine your own spiritual roots and spiritual condition. Your child's early spiritual experience is mediated through you, the parent, so you need to understand the forces that have shaped your own spiritual experience—your spiritual heritage.

To develop a clearer picture of your spiritual heritage, complete the following spiritual genogram. It may require asking questions of your parents or grandparents or aunts and uncles about your family's spiritual history. Fill out the genogram for yourself (but first photocopy or reproduce the blank genogram on a separate piece of paper) and have your spouse complete one, too.

As the Scriptures tell us, spiritual problems have a way of repeating themselves to later generations, so in order to break any unhealthy cycles, we must know what kinds of generational beliefs, attitudes, customs, habits, and sins have brought us to the point we find ourselves in today.

Completing the genogram is simple. Just write the names of each family member in the space provided, and for each person in the family, circle the spiritual traits you can validate, either from your own personal experience or from the results of interviewing family members. This will help you gain a clearer picture of your family's spiritual heritage. Use the letters below to represent your family members.

GGF	= great-grandfather	GGM	= great-grandmother
GF	= grandfather	GM	= grandmother
F	= father	M	= mother
P1	= parent (self)	P2	= other parent
( )	= name of person being rated		

The letters below represent the areas of spirituality that you will try to validate for each family member.

S   = was saved
F   = had strong, authentic faith
M   = modeled true Christianity
PR   = practiced what they preached
I   = had strong moral integrity, honesty, did not hide the truth
L   = was loving and affectionate with family members
W   = attended worship in church regularly
B   = was known for reading the Bible regularly
PP   = was known for faithfulness in prayer
FS   = consistently exhibited the fruit of the Spirit
E   = was emotionally open and expressive

Your name _____

	GGF ( )	GGM ( )	GGF ( )	GGM ( )
Saved	S	S	S	S
Faith	F	F	F	F
Modeled	M	M	M	M
Practiced	PR	PR	PR	PR
Integrity	I	I	I	I
Love	L	L	L	L
Worship	W	W	W	W
Bible	B	B	B	B
Prayer	PP	PP	PP	PP
Fruit of the Spirit	FS	FS	FS	FS
Emotional Openness	E	E	E	E

	GF ( )	GM ( )	GF ( )	GM ( )
Saved	S	S	S	S
Faith	F	F	F	F
Modeled	M	M	M	M
Practiced	PR	PR	PR	PR
Integrity	I	I	I	I
Love	L	L	L	L
Worship	W	W	W	W

Bible	B	B	B	B
Prayer	PP	PP	PP	PP
Fruit of the Spirit	FS	FS	FS	FS
Emotional Openness	E	E	E	E

		F	M	
	(	) (	)	
Saved		S	S	
Faith		F	F	
Modeled		M	M	
Practiced		PR	PR	
Integrity		I	I	
Love		L	L	
Worship		W	W	
Bible		B	B	
Prayer		PP	PP	
Fruit of the Spirit		FS	FS	
Emotional Openness		E	E	

		P1	P2	
	(	) (	)	
Saved		S	S	
Faith		F	F	
Modeled		M	M	
Practiced		PR	PR	
Integrity		I	I	
Love		L	L	
Worship		W	W	
Bible		B	B	
Prayer		PP	PP	
Fruit of the Spirit		FS	FS	
Emotional Openness		E	E	

Evaluating This Assessment

To evaluate your spiritual genogram, look at three generational patterns that emerge.

Individual Imperfections. These are traits that cannot be validated in the life of a given individual. These are not major concerns.

Generational Flaws. These are traits that cannot be validated over a period of two generations and seem to be transmitted from one generation to the next. For example, if your grandfather on your father's side and your father were both weak in the area of prayer, this would be a flaw that you may need to concentrate on correcting in yourself so you can pass on a healthy prayer heritage to your children.

Multigenerational Cycles. These are traits that cannot be validated over three or more generations. If your great-grandmother on your mother's side, your grandmother on your mother's side, and your mother were all emotionally inexpressive, then there is a greatly increased likelihood that you and your child will inherit this flaw—unless you take positive steps to break the cycle. You need to stop that cycle in it tracks right now so that your child can have a healthy, secure spiritual experience.

You will use the insights from your spiritual genogram in completing a comprehensive assessment at the end of this chapter.

Measuring Your Own Emotional Roots

YOU, THE PARENT, ARE the soil in which your child's first spiritual seeds are planted. It is important to sift that soil to discover any debris or impurities that would cause future spiritual contamination. This involves another round of emotional self-evaluation. Our emotional development is crucial because the way we are able to experience affirmation, unconditional love, and grace in childhood largely shapes how we experience and internalize God— and that, of course, strongly influences the image of God we pass on to our own children.

Place a check mark in front of each statement that expresses your experience or memory.

    ____ 1. I could trust my mother and father to love and care for me.

    ____ 2. My mother and father made me feel worthwhile.

    ____ 3. My mother and father loved me unconditionally.

    ____ 4. My mother and father were dependable when I was emotionally frustrated.

___ 5. My mother and father encouraged my independence, self-discipline, decision making, and outreach to others.

___ 6. My relationship with my mother and father made it easy for me to develop an obedient attitude and respect for authority.

___ 7. My mother and father were consistent in their love for me.

___ 8. I always saw my mother and father as being fair.

___ 9. When I was a child, I enjoyed living.

___ 10. When I was a child, I had enough special friends.

___ 11. When I was a child, I felt accepted in school.

___ 12. When I was a child, I felt equal with my peers.

___ 13. I would describe my childhood as happy.

___ 14. My mother and father paid attention to me when home.

___ 15. My mother and father were physically affectionate.

___ 16. My mother and father were verbally affectionate.

___ 17. I received regular verbal praise and affirmation from my mother and father.

___ 18. My mother and father were emotionally open.

___ 19. I could share almost anything with my mother and father.

___ 20. From an early age, I always felt forgiven by my mother and father and God when I did something wrong.

___ 21. I always felt that my mother and father were with me in spirit, though they may not have been there at times.

Evaluating This Assessment

This exercise helps you to identify developmental tasks that were not adequately completed in your own childhood and that may reflect problems in your parenting style. For instance, if you did not check statement number four, which deals with your ability to trust your parents, you may find that in your adult life, you have problems opening up emotionally to your spouse, your children, and God. You didn't feel you could trust mom and dad to help you with your emotional frustrations, so you keep your emotions closed to those around you now. You project your distrust onto God, doubting his love for you. As a result, your children may experience you as an emotionally closed person, which will negatively affect their image of God, and they may absorb your doubts and distrust.

The list below shows that the above checklist was grouped according to certain developmental tasks that we all should have accomplished in childhood but that may be an area of continuing struggle for you: security, trust, self-worth, assurance and validation, and intimacy. Place a check mark by any categories in which you were unable to check all of the statements—these are areas in which you need to work to secure your own spirituality (perhaps through counseling) so that you can more positively affect your child's spirituality.

___Security: Statements 1–4
___Trust: Statements 5–8
___Self-Worth: Statements 9–13
___Assurance and Validation: Statements 14–17
___Intimacy: Statements 18–21

Assessing Your Childhood Spiritual Security

THIS ASSESSMENT EMPLOYS THE same assessment tool we used in "Assessing Your Child's Current Spiritual Security." Place a check mark by those statements you can validate. For early stages, you may ask your parent or parents for insight into areas you were too young to remember.

As a child, I demonstrated that I

Infancy Stage (Birth to Fifteen Months)

___felt safe and secure in my parents' presence
___felt safe and secure in my parents' absence
___responded positively to parental cuddling, cooing, and
    stroking

Toddler Stage (Fifteen Months to Three Years)

___felt loved and accepted in my parents' presence
___felt loved and accepted after being left alone
___felt loved and accepted after being told no
___could freely give love verbally and physically
___started the process of separation-individuation
___was more at peace than angry
___had an acceptable attitude toward authority

Preschool (Three to Six Years)

___believed in the concept of God
___believed God is love
___believed God is good
___believed God is personal
___had the beginnings of a healthy respect and reverence for God
___believed in and trusted God's unconditional love and acceptance
___resolved guilt easily by trusting God to forgive
___formed an inner conscience
___had a natural interest in learning about spiritual concepts
___had at least a moderately positive attitude (or not a negative attitude) toward prayer and Bible time
___had a generally positive attitude toward church (setting aside normal preschool frustration and acting-out behavior)
___could practice basic obedience

Latency (Approximately Six to Twelve Years)

___had an interest in learning spiritual truths
___accepted Christ or brought up the need
___took initiative to form my own relationship with God
___had a growing confidence in God's ability to be merciful and forgive
___maintained a positive attitude toward God, his authority, and his claim on our lives

___experienced security in my faith, even during difficult times

___showed evidence of the fruit of the Spirit in daily life, as listed in Galatians 5:22–23

Adolescence (Approximately Thirteen to Twenty-one Years)

___accepted Christ or brought up the need (if this was not accomplished in the latency stage)

___was interested in fellowship with other Christian young people

___believed I was worthwhile to God

___felt God was close and available

___trusted God's grace and forgiveness

___depended on God's promises for support, inner control, and guidance

___looked to God—not self, pleasure, or materialism—for purpose and meaning in life

___was able to choose self-restraint and obedience to God's authority

___was able to make good decisions, seeking God's will (through the Holy Spirit) over self-will (the flesh)

___began to comprehend more complex spiritual concepts such as the Holy Spirit and the Trinity

___was able to openly initiate the confession of sin

___began to act on the truths of the Bible

___demonstrated an interest in the Christian life that superseded an interest in cultural deceptions such as materialism and secularism

___was self-motivated to worship God in a church setting

___independently sought a prayer life and devotional life outside the church worship experience

___demonstrated the fruit of the Spirit in a meaningful and daily-increasing way

___could internalize Scripture texts of wisdom and assurance, finding them useful and personally meaningful

___could easily internalize (feel) God's love, finding his love to be real, personal, and meaningful

___could love with both friendship love and Christlike, unconditional love
___demonstrated a willingness and ability to forgive others
___rarely doubted my salvation
___could relate to God on a personal level

Evaluating This Assessment

This assessment shows you where some of the cracks in your own spiritual and developmental foundation may have formed earlier in your life. Any item not checked is, in essence, a stress fracture in your spiritual security. The earlier the stage in which it occurred, the more damage it caused to later development.

If you have areas in which you need to work on repairing your foundation and completing developmental tasks not adequately mastered in childhood, consider working through these areas with a professional Christian therapist.

Assessing Your Present Spiritual Security

PLACE A CHECK MARK in front of each statement that expresses your current feelings. Answer these questions on the basis of your true feelings, not on the basis of what you have been taught or what you "ought" to think or what is "doctrinally correct." The issue you are trying to get at in this assessment is the state of your emotions, not your doctrinal position.

___ 1. Sometimes I do not feel comfortable praying to God.
___ 2. At times it is emotionally hard for me to read the Bible.
___ 3. I often feel alienated from God.
___ 4. I would honestly have to admit that at some level I feel resentment toward God.
___ 5. I cannot trust God as much as I would like to.
___ 6. I sometimes have difficulty experiencing God's unconditional love and acceptance.
___ 7. I sometimes do not feel God loves me.
___ 8. I sometimes feel God must be punishing me.

___ 9. I would be embarrassed if anyone knew how I actually feel about God.

___ 10. I feel some anxiety or apprehension about going to church.

___ 11. I must honestly admit feeling spiritually empty for a long time.

___ 12. I have trouble relating to God on a personal level.

___ 13. I frequently doubt my salvation.

___ 14. Though I call myself a Christian, I inwardly question God's personal nature more than I am willing to admit.

___ 15. I feel God expects me to be perfect, and I can never be perfect.

___ 16. I often question God's fairness.

___ 17. At times I have trouble accepting God's complete forgiveness.

___ 18. At times I feel God has abandoned me and that he is nowhere to be found.

___ 19. Someone in my past has caused me to stumble spiritually, and I have had difficulty regaining my spiritual stability.

___ 20. I divide God's character into traits I like and traits I dislike.

___ 21. God is responsible for most of the suffering I experience in my life.

___ 22. I have sinned greatly, and I feel I cannot go back to church.

___ 23. The church is full of hypocrites. I don't want to be around people who claim to know God but do not live like it.

___ 24. When I think of church, I feel anxious.

___ 25. I feel God loves me when I perform up to certain standards and doesn't accept me when I fail.

___ 26. Most of the time I walk in the flesh rather than the Spirit.

___ 27. I am not sure if I can count on my faith to get me through the valleys in my life.

___ 28. How I have experienced God in my life has not been in line with what I was taught or what I believe about God.

___ 29. I know about the fruit of the Spirit, but rarely in my daily life do I experience "love, joy, peace, patience, kindness, goodness, faithfulness, gentleness and self-control" with any consistency.

___ 30. Sometimes I wonder what the use of praying is, and I feel it doesn't change anything.

Evaluating This Assessment

Now count the number of check marks. A zero would be absolute perfection. If you scored a perfect zero on this assessment, you scored better than I did! A score of zero would indicate that you have absolutely perfect spiritual security—no questions, no doubts, no problems, no spiritual contamination of any kind. Most people, even under the best of spiritual circumstances, would honestly have to check a few of these statements. Remember, this exercise is designed to test not your theology but your feelings. You are not being graded. You are trying to discover insight into your own personality.

Anyone is bound to experience some stress or doubt regarding a personal relationship with God. So a score from 2 to 10 would indicate a fairly healthy spiritual security—some areas of struggle, some areas of tension, some questions that are honestly being faced as part of the process of growing more mature as a Christian.

If you scored from 11 to 20, you are probably experiencing some significant spiritual insecurity. You have some genuine hurts and fractures in your early spiritual foundation that need to be addressed, possibly through counseling with a Christian therapist. These hurts and questions are interfering with the way you understand, experience, and relate to God. Scoring in this range indicates that you probably have a history of both positive and negative experiences with God. You may have received some inconsistent messages about God in childhood—either direct messages, such as "God won't love you if you do that," or indirect messages, in the form of parents or other caregivers who did not consistently model godly love and acceptance to you. These inconsistent messages about God continue to reverberate within you in adulthood, creating a noticeable dissonance between what you *think* about God and what you *feel* toward God.

If you scored more than 21, you are likely spiritually handicapped. But please understand this: there is no shame in having a broken spiritual foundation. You can resupport that foundation, and you can experience a stronger faith and an intimate and vital relationship with God, through working on your spiritual and emotional issues. This certainly does not mean you are not saved, nor does it mean you are not a good person. It simply means that you didn't receive the emotional support everyone needs in childhood, and your relationship with God is not as rich and satisfying as it can be—and as it must be, in order to pass on a healthy experience of God to your children. If this is your situation, I would urge you to obtain counseling with a Christian therapist; that therapist may also be able to recommend a Christian support group that can increase your level of insight and accelerate your spiritual healing.

There are ten basic misconceptions that people tend to experience regarding God, and you may have discovered some of these misconceptions in your own experience as you completed the preceding assessment.

God has good and bad traits. Many people relate to God as if he were a human being, possessing desirable and undesirable traits. They compartmentalize his attributes and say, "I like some things about God, and I dislike others." Others say, "I know God loves everyone, he's a personal God. But he's also all seeing and knowing, and that makes me feel like he's always looking over my shoulder waiting to nail me for a mistake."

Clearly the Bible leaves no room for sidestepping this issue: God is entirely good and has no bad traits whatsoever. Most people find it easier to believe what the Bible says about the goodness of God than to feel and experience it on a moment-by-moment basis—particularly if they are going through a painful trial. Our goal must be to bring our feelings about God into conformity with who God really is.

God is undependable. Many people find it difficult to put their entire trust in God. They feel that God does not always hear them when they pray. Or they believe that God sometimes reneges on the promises he made in the Bible. This distrust in God most often occurs when we develop unrealistic expectations about God. We believe that God will grant us anything we ask for, or that if we ask it in the name of Jesus he will protect us from all harm and suffering. The truth is, God never promised us there would be no more suffering. When we come to a realistic expectation of God that is in line with Scripture, we can then be assured that God is dependable and that we can trust him with every detail of our lives.

God is unfair. This is one of the most common complaints against God: "If you are just, loving, and all-powerful, God, why do you allow suffering?" and, "Why does God allow evil people to abuse innocent children, then get off scot-free?" These feelings are understandable, given the massive injustices that go on around us. Yet the Bible makes it plain that God is just, even though evil reigns in this world. A time will come when God's justice and wisdom will be made known to all of us who love him as well as to those who do evil.

God is a religious institution. Many people mistakenly identify the institutional church with God himself. When a pastor or spiritual leader goes bad, God in turn becomes bad. While it is true that the church is God's representative on earth, it is made up of imperfect human beings who do not always represent the nature of God. The church is a reflection of our image of who God is, and sometimes that reflection can become distorted. The institutional church should never be confused with God himself.

God is a controller. Many people feel that if they commit their lives to God, he will take away their happiness, freedom, and choices. The issue of control presents us with a beautiful spiritual paradox: the Bible urges us to give our lives over to God's control, yet God is not a controller! He never forces us or manipulates us into doing anything, although he knows we can never be happy and fulfilled apart from him. God does want to guide us and protect us, but he will never take our free will away.

God is too demanding. Many people see God as a cosmic critic, always looking over our shoulder, always saying, "Not good enough." This distorted image of God can lead to religious addiction—the compulsive need to do religious work to the point of exhaustion and burnout. People who see God as a demanding critic have set their expectations higher than God's. They feel that God's yoke on them is heavy, which results in depression, spiritual defeat, and emotional paralysis. The truth is, Jesus came to give comfort to the weary and defeated, and to introduce them to a God who is accepting, not demanding. Jesus said, "Come to me, all you who are weary and burdened, and I will give you rest. . . . For my yoke is easy and my burden is light" (Matt. 11:28, 30).

A personal God does not exist. There are those who believe that although there may be some kind of god, he (or it) is not a personal god. When Einstein was asked if he believed in God, he replied that he believed in a god that was nothing more or less than the sum of all the laws of the universe. He did not believe that this god was personally involved with human beings. Many other people believe in a god that is a vague power (like the Force in George Lucas's *Star Wars* movies). Still others struggle with the desire to believe in a God they cannot see, touch, hear, or feel. This is a particular problem for people who were abandoned or neglected as children. All of these conceptions are variations on the theme that God, as a personal, relational being, does not exist. The sources of these false perceptions of God are varied. Some come from liberal theory or New Age mysticism, others come into our minds when we fail to understand God's Word accurately. The Bible teaches us that, in spite of our beliefs and theories about God, he is real, he is personal, and he is involved in our lives.

God is a critical parent or a condemning judge. Many people see God as a critical parent standing over them with a big hickory switch, just waiting for them to get out of line. Others see God as a grim judge in black robes, and fear that he will condemn them to a life sentence—or even an eternity—of suffering for breaking one of his laws. The Bible teaches that God is love. Only good things come from God, and while God hates sin, he loves sinners. He doesn't want to punish, but to restore broken souls.

God holds grudges. Some people see God as a cold and unforgiving deity who is just waiting to pay us back for our sins. They picture him keeping a list of wrongs to be presented as evidence against us on Judgment Day. Some wrongs he never forgets and never forgives. Commit a "really bad" sin and God will turn his back on you.

This is not the God of the Bible. The God of the Bible is described as One of great love and mercy who will not remember our sins if we confess them to him.

God is not holy and perfect. Christianity has become so secularized and institutionalized that many people today have little understanding of what holiness really means. Even among professing Christians, we frequently encounter irreverent jokes, an indulgent attitude toward sin, and a sense that God is just "one of the boys." God is gracious, loving, forgiving, and personal, but we should never forget that he is also *holy*. Holiness, as it refers to God, means perfection and purity—an immaculate spotlessness. In God there is not the slightest hint or shadow of sin, not the faintest evil motive.

Assessing Your Image of God

THE NEXT EXERCISE IS a list of attributes (traits or character qualities) that might be applied to God, according to your experience. Again, this is not a checklist to determine if you are "theologically correct." This is a checklist to help you better understand your emotions and experience of God, so try to reach deep within your feelings as you mark your answers.

For each item, place a check by one letter that most closely describes how you feel about and experience God.

1. I most often feel that God is
   __a. condemning __b. objective __c. forgiving and merciful

2. In my experience, I have found God to be
   __a. neutral __b. fair and just __c. partial and biased

3. I most often feel that God is
   __a. involved __b. asleep __c. observant

4. Throughout my life, I have tended to experience God as
   __a. demanding __b. considerate __c. loving

5. I tend to view God as
   __a. omnipotent and perfect __b. capable and consistent
   __c. limited and fallible

6. I most often relate to God as a
   __a. higher power __b. friend __c. father

7. I most often feel that God is
   __a. insensitive __b. available __c. nurturing

8. I most often feel that God is a
   __a. role model __b. deliverer __c. disciplinarian

9. In my experience, I have found God to be
   __a. unreliable __b. trustworthy __c. responsible

10. I tend to view God as
    __a. real __b. believable __c. imaginary

11. I tend to feel that God is
    __a. understanding and approachable __b. empathetic and
    touchable __c. aloof and distant

12. I generally see God as
    __a. a dictator __b. Lord __c. an authority

Evaluating This Assessment

On the checklist, each multiple choice answer is assigned a point value between 1 and 3. Below is a key that lists the point values for each answer. You are not being graded; there is no pass or fail. This is a diagnostic tool, and the purpose of this assessment is to help you to evaluate your own image of God.

1.	a = 1	b = 2	c = 3
2.	a = 2	b = 3	c = 1
3.	a = 3	b = 1	c = 2
4.	a = 1	b = 2	c = 3
5.	a = 3	b = 2	c = 1

6. a = 1   b = 2   c = 3
7. a = 1   b = 2   c = 3
8. a = 2   b = 3   c = 1
9. a = 1   b = 3   c = 2
10. a = 3   b = 2   c = 1
11. a = 2   b = 3   c = 1
12. a = 1   b = 3   c = 2

If you scored from 12 to 21, you are probably experiencing God in a negative way, as someone who is nonloving and even threatening. The attributes you selected tend to be unfavorable, which would indicate that distortions are likely in your image of God and in your relationship with God.

If you scored from 22 to 29, you probably hold a safe and neutral position on who God is. You may be avoiding intimacy with God by riding the fence. That is especially true if you tended to select several attributes with a point value of 2.

If your answers tended to be a fairly even mix of 1s, 2s, and 3s, you likely feel ambivalent or uncertain in your experience with God. Perhaps you hesitate to admit all of the negative feelings you have toward God—feelings you hold now or have experienced in the past. Another possible interpretation is that you may hesitate to accept the concept of a perfect and holy God.

If you scored 30 or above, you selected attributes reflecting a healthy, biblical concept of a perfect, holy, forgiving, loving God.

Did you have a difficult time with the checklist? Do not worry. Most people do! Choosing just one attribute that most consistently describes your view of some aspect of God's character can be frustrating. We all go through changes and moods and different experiences. At times, we may feel God is understanding—even empathetic, like a close friend. At other times, we may feel that God has removed himself from us and that when we pray, we pray to an empty sky. Most of us maintain positive and negative views of God at different times. If forced to choose, many people with a negative perception of God will select a neutral attribute, because they tend to feel guilty otherwise.

You may have noticed a tension and frustration within your-self as you completed the checklist. If so, you have encountered—at the level of your feelings—one of the key principles of this book: *A healthy image of God and a healthy relationship with God result when our feelings about God are the most consistent with our bib-lically based beliefs about God.* Here is how the Bible describes God's true nature.

He is loving

The LORD appeared to us in the past, saying: "I have loved you with an everlasting love; I have drawn you with loving-kindness."

Jeremiah 31:3

"For God so loved the world that he gave his one and only Son, that whoever believes in him shall not perish but have eternal life."

John 3:16

He is forgiving

"Come now, let us reason together," says the LORD. "Though your sins are like scarlet, they shall be as white as snow; though they are red as crimson, they shall be like wool."

Isaiah 1:18

At dawn he appeared again in the temple courts, where all the people gathered around him, and he sat down to teach them. The teachers of the law and the Pharisees brought in a woman caught in adultery. They made her stand before the group and said to Jesus, "Teacher, this woman was caught in the act of adultery. In the Law Moses commanded us to stone such women. Now what do you say?" They were using this question as a trap, in order to have a basis for accusing him.

But Jesus bent down and started to write on the ground with his finger. When they kept on questioning him, he straightened up and said to them, "If any one of you is without sin, let him be the first to throw a stone at her." Again he stooped down and wrote on the ground.

At this, those who heard began to go away one at a time, the older ones first, until only Jesus was left, with the woman still standing there. Jesus straightened up and asked her, "Woman, where are they? Has no one condemned you?"

"No one, sir," she said.

"Then neither do I condemn you," Jesus declared. "Go now and leave your life of sin."

John 8:2–11

He is gracious and accepting

For all have sinned and fall short of the glory of God, and are justified freely by his grace through the redemption that came by Christ Jesus.

Romans 3:23–24

"All that the Father gives me will come to me, and whoever comes to me I will never drive away."

John 6:37

He is merciful

Give thanks to the LORD, for he is good;
　　his love endures forever.
Let Israel say:
　　"His love endures forever."
Let the house of Aaron say:
　　"His love endures forever."
Let those who fear the LORD say:
　　"His love endures forever."

Psalm 118:1–4

Praise be to the God and Father of our Lord Jesus Christ, the Father of compassion and the God of all comfort.

2 Corinthians 1:3

He is personal

The word of the LORD came to me, saying, "Before I formed you in the womb I knew you, before you were born I set you apart; I appointed you as a prophet to the nations."

Jeremiah 1:4–5

O LORD, you have searched me
  and you know me.
You know when I sit and when I rise;
  you perceive my thoughts from afar.

Psalm 139:1–2

He is faithful

Know therefore that the LORD your God is God; he is the faithful God, keeping his covenant of love to a thousand generations of those who love him and keep his commands.

Deuteronomy 7:9

Your love, O LORD, reaches to the heavens,
  your faithfulness to the skies.
Your righteousness is like the mighty mountains,
  your justice like the great deep.

Psalm 36:5–6

He is the source of peace

I will lie down and sleep in peace,
  for you alone, O LORD,
  make me dwell in safety.

Psalm 4:8

You will keep in perfect peace
    him whose mind is steadfast,
    because he trusts in you.

Isaiah 26:3

He is our loving Father

A father to the fatherless, a defender of widows,
    is God in his holy dwelling.

Psalm 68:5

"Do not be afraid, little flock, for your Father has been pleased to give you the kingdom."

Luke 12:32

He is perfect

I will proclaim the name of the LORD.
    Oh, praise the greatness of our God!
He is the Rock, his works are perfect,
    and all his ways are just.
A faithful God who does no wrong,
    upright and just is he.

Deuteronomy 32:3–4

Every good and perfect gift is from above, coming down from the Father of the heavenly lights, who does not change like shifting shadows.

James 1:17

He is trustworthy

But let all who take refuge in you be glad;
    let them ever sing for joy.
Spread your protection over them,
    that those who love your name may rejoice in you.

For surely, O LORD, you bless the righteous;
  you surround them with your favor as with a shield.

Psalm 5:11–12

Taste and see that the LORD is good;
  blessed is the man who takes refuge in him.
Fear the LORD, you his saints,
  for those who fear him lack nothing.
The lions may grow weak and hungry,
  but those who seek the LORD lack no good thing.

Psalm 34:8–10

Making Constructive Changes

YOU HAVE JUST TAKEN a snapshot of your child, yourself, and your family background and traditions, through six assessment tools, focusing on

- your child's current spiritual security
- your spiritual heritage (spiritual genogram)
- your own childhood emotional development
- your own childhood spiritual security
- your own current spiritual security
- your image of God

In "Assessing Your Child's Current Spiritual Security," you evaluated your child's present spiritual condition at his stage and age level. Place a check mark by the stage at which you assessed your child's spiritual security.

___Infancy
___Toddler
___Preschool
___Latency
___Adolescence

Now identify below any significant spiritual growth tasks your child failed to achieve by the time of your assessment, and then write down one or two actions you intend to take in order to strengthen your child's spiritual security. For example, if you write under "Failed task," *My child seems unsure of God's unconditional love*, you might write under "Action I will take," *I will demonstrate unconditional love, hugging and expressing love to him often, especially after disciplining him; I will tell him about God's unconditional love and teach him Scripture verses such as Jeremiah 31:3 and John 3:16.*

Failed task: _____

Action I will take:_____

_____

Failed task: _____

Action I will take:_____

_____

Failed task: _____

Action I will take:_____

_____

In "Where Are You Spiritually?" you filled out a spiritual genogram for four generations of your family history. Using the insight you gained from your genogram, list any flaws you discovered in your family's spiritual heritage (for example, *lack of faith, lack of Christian models, lack of integrity on father's side*, or *lack of love and fruit of the Spirit on mother's side*).

_____

_____

_____

_____

_____

_____

Now list some actions you intend to take in order to repair those flaws and break the intergenerational cycle so that those flaws will not be passed on to your children (for example, *I will ask my*

Bible study group to hold me accountable to demonstrate integrity and live out my faith on a daily basis, or I will seek counseling for help in dealing with the poisonous emotional residue from an abusive past, or I will encourage my children to share their feelings with me, and I will model emotional openness by appropriately sharing my own feelings with them).

_____

_____

_____

_____

_____

Note: Repeat this process for any individual imperfections or multi-generational cycles you discovered in your spiritual genogram.

In "Measuring Your Own Spiritual and Emotional Roots," you evaluated your childhood emotional development and rated your progress in five categories of emotional development—security, trust, self-worth, assurance and validation, and intimacy. In the space below, explain how each incomplete emotional task in your own life has adversely affected your child's spiritual and emotional development.

_____

_____

_____

_____

_____

Now write down the specific steps you will take to repair the damage to your own spiritual and emotional development and to prevent or repair damage to your child's spiritual and emotional development.

_____

_____

_____

_____

_____

_____

In "Assessing Your Childhood Spiritual Security," you examined your own childhood at different stages of spiritual growth and development. In the space below, list any significant childhood spiritual tasks you did not complete.

Infancy: _____

_____

Toddler: _____

_____

Preschool:_____

_____

Latency: _____

_____

Adolescence:_____

_____

What specific steps will you take to complete those tasks and to fill in the gaps of your spiritual development?

_____

_____

_____

_____

_____

In "Assessing Your Present Spiritual Security," you answered a series of questions that evaluated your level of spiritual security. Having interpreted your score, write down what you discovered about yourself and your relationship with God. Are you spiritually secure, insecure, or handicapped? What impact has your level of spiritual security or insecurity had on your child's spiritual development?

_____

_____

_____

_____

_____

In "Assessing Your Image of God," you looked at the attributes of God in terms of your image of him. Having interpreted your score, write down in the space below what you discovered about your image of God. Was it positive and healthy, neutral, or extremely distorted? How does your image of God compare with the Bible's portrayal of God, as listed on pages 218 to 222?

_____

_____

_____

_____

_____

Do you think that your image of God has had a positive or negative impact on your child's image of God?

If positive, in what way?

_____

_____

_____

_____

_____

If negative, in what way?

_____

_____

_____

_____

_____

_____

What specific distortions in your image of God do you need to change so that your feelings come into conformity with the Bible's portrayal of who God is? (For example, *I imagine God as a critical judge; the Bible says that God is merciful,* or *I see God as distant, but the Bible says he is close and available*.) And what specific actions do you plan to take in order to build a strong, healthy, biblically based image of God in your child?

_____

_____

_____

_____

_____

_____

Remember that your child's spiritual development is deeply linked to his emotional development. Mental or cognitive approaches to encouraging your child's spiritual development (Bible reading, Bible discussion, Bible memorization, and the like) are important. But never neglect or underestimate the importance of emotional and experiential approaches to spiritual development: providing a loving, forgiving home atmosphere; conveying affirmation and affection through hugs, play, and affectionate touch; frequent eye communication; linking discipline to hugs and other expressions of unconditional love; sharing feelings; and so forth.

You have written down a series of action steps for healing your own spiritual hurts and encouraging your child's spiritual growth. Here are some suggestions that may help you in carrying them out over time. Find a trusted Christian friend (or a group of friends, such as a parents' support group at your church) to share those goals with. Ask your friend or friends to hold you accountable and to check in with you on a daily or weekly basis and ask you how you are progressing toward your goals. Be honest when you fail; forgive yourself and ask those who hold you accountable to forgive you and to pray with you and for you as you renew your commitment to be the kind of Christian parent God wants you to be. If necessary, take these issues to a pastor-counselor or a Christian therapist (professional counseling is especially important if there is a history of abuse or some other deep emotional wound in your background).

Christian parents today deserve a spiritual medal of honor. It is not easy to raise godly, spiritually secure kids in the face of the cultural decline and moral depravity of today's world—and it will be much harder in the even more perilous conditions that appear to be on the horizon as we move into the next century. To raise children with a sound emotional, psychological, and spiritual foundation requires that parents themselves do a lot of emotional, psychological, and spiritual housecleaning. It may require time spent in support groups or counseling. It certainly demands a great deal of care, prayer, and thought.

As Christian parents, our goal must go beyond merely imparting a conceptual, theoretical, or theological religion to our children. Our children need a relationship with God, an experience with God, that is secure, personal, powerful, meaningful, and practical. They need a faith that works in the trenches, not just in the pews. We must be willing to do anything, make any sacrifice, explore any avenue—including the pain and failings of our own past—in order to provide a healthy environment for such a real and personal faith to grow.

EPILOGUE:

The Not-Too-Distant Future

A large group of mourners were crowded into the living room of Hanna's small home. There was no casket, no urn. There were no flowers, nor was there any organ music. Michael—now a lean, graying man in his forties—stood to speak.

"Thank you all for coming," he said. "The world has changed a great deal in my father's lifetime. When J. W. Brown came into the world, back in the 1940s, the nations of the world were at war with each other. Today there are no nations, just a one-world government. The constitution he grew up under, which guaranteed freedom of religion, has been replaced by a world charter, which guarantees freedom *from* religion. The Lord we worship has been outlawed. We are assembled in my sister's home to honor my father's memory, because the law does not allow us to assemble in a Christian church. But even though our faith can no longer be practiced openly, our faith is strong, our trust in God is sure. We know that J. W. Brown was a man who walked with God, and we know he has gone home to be with his Lord. When my father died, his life was not ended. It was *completed*. And I thank God for my father."

Sitting on the sofa behind Michael, Hanna watched her brother speak, her eyes glistening. Beside Hanna were her husband, Scott, and her daughter, Jenea, now a grown young woman with a husband and child of her own.

"J. W. Brown was not a perfect man," Michael continued, "but he was a great example to me, especially in his later years, of what a Christian is supposed to be. He taught me how to live with integrity and courage, how to forgive and seek forgiveness, how to love, and how to show mercy. When I strayed from the faith, he humbled himself and loved me back into the kingdom. My father truly showed me how to live. And in these last few days, he has shown me how to die."

Michael's two boys—fourteen-year-old Joshua and eleven-year-old Caleb—sat on the floor at his feet, arms loosely wrapped about their knees, their eyes serious as they listened to their father speak. "Dad suffered physically during his last days on earth," Michael continued, "yet he suffered with quiet courage and dignity. As you know, the health care system refuses to treat cancer patients in their seventies. It offers people like my father only two options: euthanasia or suffering. My father chose to live out the days God had given him, even with the pain, rather than accept a suicide pill from the world government. He used those final days to write a letter, and he asked me to read the letter to you all at this memorial service."

Michael took a pair of reading glasses from his pocket and adjusted them on the bridge of his nose, then unfolded three handwritten pages and began to read.

My Friends,

By the time you hear these words, I will be in the presence of the Lord. The world I'm going to is a much better world than the one in which you must live. But I believe it is only a short time before the Lord returns to set wrong to right, and to restore his kingdom on earth. Soon, very soon, we will all be together again.

Meanwhile, I have a few things to say to you all. First, I want to thank God for my family. Joanna, my dear wife, who went to be with the Lord two years ago, discovered late in life—just as I did—that God is not only a Judge but a loving and merciful Father. She was a faithful friend and partner, and I am eager to join her in eternity.

My daughter, Hanna, taught me more about being a Christian parent than I ever taught her. Somehow she survived the poor example I set, and she was able to experience God as the loving and merciful Father he truly is—and then she introduced this loving, merciful Father to me. I watched how she and her husband, Scott, parented their little girl, Jenea, with love and affirmation instead of fear and scolding. From them, I saw the mistakes I had made as a parent—and I learned how to apologize and make amends for those mistakes. Hanna broke the cycle of pain that had been a Brown family tradition for generations—and she showed me how to break that cycle, too.

Jenea has grown to be a lovely Christian young woman. She and her husband, Nathan, are raising their daughter, Faith, in the nurture and admonition of the Lord. That phrase—"nurture and admonition"—has become very real and meaningful to me as I have watched Jenea and Nathan care for their little girl. When I was a father with little ones in my house, I understood how to admonish my children. I didn't know how to nurture them. But praise God, Faith is being brought up to understand not only the law of God but the love of God, not only the admonition of God but the nurture of God.

I'm thankful for my son, Mike. I drove him away from the faith for a while, but he came back and he forgave me. The Lord has given him a strong faith and has used Mike to reach many people for Christ. The thrill of my life was to see my son become a pastor. Of course, there's no place for Mike in the World Church, with its mixture of watered-down Christianity, Hinduism, Buddhism, and occultism, so he can't earn a living as a pastor anymore. But I'm proud of his courage, for despite all the obstacles and threats he faces, both from the government and from the world around him, he never stops telling people about the Lord Jesus Christ.

Mike is raising his boys, Joshua and Caleb, to be strong in the faith—strong like their father, and strong like their biblical namesakes. I am proud of Mike, of his wife, Sara, and of the two grandsons they have given me. May God grant them, and all of my family and friends, grace for the dark days ahead.

Don't be sad for me. Instead, pray for each other, strengthen each other, hold each other close, and be of good courage. Jesus is risen, God is powerful, and nothing can separate you from his love. This is the Brown family tradition now—a tradition of faith, hope, and love. Most of all, love. I truly love you all, and my last thoughts are with you and for you, my family and my friends. Until we meet again, grace and peace.

In the name of Jesus,
J. W. Brown

Michael carefully refolded the papers and tucked them away in his battered old Bible. "That was my father's last will and testament," he said, "a testament of faith, a testament of love, a testament of hope. We don't know what tomorrow holds. We don't know if the Lord will return for us today or next year or a thousand years from now. We believe the signs are right for the return of Jesus any day now—but so did the believers in the first-century church. Only God truly knows the day and hour of his return. Our job is to be faithful and obedient until that time comes."

Michael turned to his niece, Jenea, who held a beautiful one-year-old daughter in her lap. "May I hold her?" he asked. Jenea lifted the child, and Michael took her and held her up before all the people who were crowded into that room. "This," he said, "is J. W. Brown's great-granddaughter, and her name, appropriately enough, is Faith. My father was able to see and hold his great-granddaughter before he died. One of the last things he told me was, 'Tell them to love their children.' He wanted me to tell you all to hold your children tightly, to surround them with your love, to meet their emotional needs, to help them feel as secure as possible despite these insecure and uncertain times. He wanted me to tell you that you are God's representative to your children. They receive God's hugs from your arms. They sense God's loving heart through your voice and your touch."

As Michael held her, Faith reached up and touched his face, cooing contentedly. "There is an old saying," Michael concluded, "'We don't know what the future holds, but we know who holds the future.' It's true. Our God holds the future, and he holds the lives and hearts of these little ones in his hands. Our job is to love them as he loves them, teach them as he would teach them, nurture them as he would nurture them. That was J. W.'s last prayer for his children and grandchildren and great-grandchildren. It is a prayer that echoes the heartbeat of our Lord, who said, 'Let the little children come to me, and do not hinder them, for the kingdom of God belongs to such as these.'"

Endnotes

Chapter Two: Spiritual Seedlings

1. Kenneth S. Kantzer, "Building Faith: How a Child Learns to Love God," *Christianity Today* 30, no. 9 (June 13, 1986), 1–7.

2. Paul Warren, *My Infant: Off to a Good Start* (Nashville: Nelson, 1994), 17.

Chapter Three: The Power of a Parent's Spiritual Character

1. William Martin, *A Prophet with Honor: The Billy Graham Story* (New York: William Morrow, 1991), 59.

2. Herbert Lockyer, *All the Women of the Bible* (Grand Rapids: Zondervan, 1988), 94.

3. Gloria Gaither, ed., *What My Parents Did Right*, (Nashville: Star Song, 1991), 68–69.

Chapter Six: The Four Dimensions of Spiritual Growth

1. James Fowler, *Stages of Faith* (San Francisco: Harper & Row, 1981).

2. Eric Erickson, *Identity and the Life Cycle* (San Francisco: International Universities Press, 1959), 65.

3. Lucy Bergman, *Through the Landscape of Faith* (Philadelphia: Westminster Press, 1986), 87.

4. David J. Loomis, "Imagination and Faith Development," *Religious Education* 83 (Spring 1988), 163–251.

Chapter Seven: Total Personality and Emotional Growth

1. Alfred Adler, *Superiority and Social Interest* (Evanston, Ill.: Northwestern University Press, 1964), 100.

For more information on child development, spiritual growth, or seminars on faith development, call or write:

Dr. Larry Stephens
The Minirth Clinic
2100 North Collins Blvd., Suite 200
Richardson, Texas 75080
(972) 669–1733

We want to hear from you. Please send your comments about this book to us in care of the address below. Thank you.

ZondervanPublishingHouse
Grand Rapids, Michigan 49530
http://www.zondervan.com